INSIDE THE MINDS

Trust and Probate Litigation

Leading Lawyers on Managing Client Expectations, Handling Complex Cases, and Navigating Recent Legal Developments

ASPATORE

Mat #41086541

Inside the Minds Project Manager, Caitlin Keiper; edited by Michaela Falls; proofread by Melanie Zimmerman

Aspatore books may be purchased for educational, business, or sales promotional use. For information, please e-mail West.customer.service@thomson.com.

ISBN 978-0-314-27079-5

For corrections, updates, comments or any other inquiries please e-mail
TLR.AspatoreEditorial@thomson.com.

First Printing, 2010
10 9 8 7 6 5 4 3 2 1

Contents

A Look at Complex Issues in the Trust and Probate Arena

Colleen Chinlund

Partner

Arnstein & Lehr LLP

ASPATORE

Introduction

Over the past eleven years, I have enjoyed a well-rounded law practice with a specialty in estate planning, probate and trust administration. When I began my law career, it became immediately apparent that a focus on estate planning involved many other facets of the law, such as corporate and real estate. Therefore, in order to address the general needs of a client, I took the necessary steps to get involved in other relevant law specialties to gain a broad knowledge base to properly service our diverse clientele. Although I no longer handle these issues directly, I am proficient in spotting the issues and developing a strategy and solution tailored for the client.

Recent Cases in Trust and Probate Law

Unfortunately, I find that case law in the trust and probate arena is very sparse. Unless there are significant assets at stake, the motivation to appeal any given ruling is simply not there. There was, however, a very relevant case related to attorneys' fees. Clients are very sensitive to the costs associated with probate and trust administration. The sympathy card played is that fees take away from their inheritance—what their loved one would have wanted them to have. Unlike other practice areas, probate attorneys may have their fees scrutinized by the court. This is a benefit to the client in that the court has oversight to determine what fees are considered "reasonable" during the administration. 755 ILCS 5/28-1. Because there is court oversight, probate attorneys need to be mindful of the descriptions of the services rendered when recording their time. Although there are many factors to consider in determining what constitutes a "reasonable fee," the judges have become very particular as to the specificity of the time recorded. Many judges will reduce fees and negate time entries altogether simply because the attorney's time entry was either vague or consisted of block billing or entries that did not set forth with specificity what was actually done, or at least what was done to benefit the estate, all of which are in complete contradiction of the precepts contained in *Kaiser v. MEPC American Properties Inc.*, 164 Ill App. 3d 978 (1st Dist. 1987) ("it is incumbent upon the petitioner to present detailed records maintained during the course of litigation containing facts upon which the charges are predicated"). In order to prevent a fee reduction or scrutiny by the client and the court, review the Kaiser case and conform your time entries accordingly. A more recent case that espouses the views of Kaiser is the Estate of Bitoy, providing additional guidance for attorneys on how to manage and record their time in order to get paid. *In re Estate of Earl Eugene Bitoy*, 395 Ill.App.3d 262 (Ill. App. 1 Dist. 2009).

The Impact of the Economy and Other Trends in Trust and Probate Litigation

A major impact of the current economic state relates to the valuation of estate assets. The impact of the economy on the value of assets is staggering and hasn't necessarily set in for family members. With respect to a privately owned family business, the family always seems to think that the business is worth much more than it actually is and become hugely disappointed because there is either no market for the sale of the business or because its productivity has unknowingly decreased because of the market conditions, making it difficult to sustain. Another aspect is the lost benefits of a step-up in basis. We are finding many assets are valued at less than the basis, causing the family to lose the benefits of any built-up gains that existed not long ago in the various investment accounts.

Increasingly, perhaps because of the economy, I am finding that people are willing to forego spending the money to have an estate plan prepared and are therefore dying without estate plans in place. As a result, we are seeing an increase in probate administration. The phrase "penny wise, pound foolish" completely summarizes the result here. The relatively nominal cost to put an estate plan in place will save in the long run by avoiding a probate administration. Probate is timely and costly and may create unnecessary limitations on the family's access to funds at a time when they may need it most. This delay is a result of statutory timelines that must be complied with—i.e., an estate may not be closed for six months from the date of publication in order to provide creditors an opportunity to file claims in the estate. Additionally, each of the heirs may have a different perspective as to how an estate should be administered or how the assets should be distributed, which can result in litigation, which creates additional costs and delays. Another issue in an intestate estate is determining heirship. Depending on the number of heirs, their relationship with the decedent, and their location, many issues will come into play not only with respect to the difficulty in getting an heirship established, but also in dealing with heirs in general. We have handled many estates where none of the heirs ever even knew the decedent and are completely unsympathetic to the situation or the process and only care about when they will receive their check. Some of these eager beneficiaries place constant demands on the administrator's attorney to circumvent the probate process. For the unsophisticated attorney who does not specialize in probate, many of the nuances relevant to an administration may be lost, causing a breach of fiduciary duties and possibly resulting in unnecessary litigation. For any executor or administrator, the best advice is to retain an attorney who specializes in probate. Not only will it save the estate time, but it will also save the estate money, especially now when it means the most to the heirs.

Common Settlement Structures

In Cook County, we have a dedicated judge who specifically deals with mediation in trust and probate cases. Therefore, whenever litigation or a contentious matter occurs, we find that probate judges are very willing to send it over to mediation—a process that is usually very successful since it avoids the high cost of litigation, although not always the case since this mediation is not binding. Unfortunately, there is no single direct settlement structure that seems to work in every case, simply because the probate process involves many aspects that are very emotional as it relates to the personal perspective of each party involved. However, mediation can definitely play a major role in advancing the parties to settlement.

One aspect of the probate process that seems to be very successful in streamlining litigation and reaching an immediate result is using a citation to discover and recover assets. The Probate Court is a court of general jurisdiction and therefore a multitude of issues related to an estate may be handled in probate in lieu of the party filing an additional suit in either the Law or Chancery Division, which will save time and mitigate costs. The procedure of a citation will cover any issues related to property and the ownership of same. The process is streamlined by filing the citation, having it issued, and then serving the parties to appear. Often, the other party is willing to settle to avoid coming into court. With respect to financial institutions, there are times when the process takes too long to liquidate an account—the required documents have been provided to the institution many times and yet the institution fails to liquidate and distribute the account. A huge motivator is serving the institution with a citation. I find this to be a very successful resource to bring institutions in conformity with the requirements of the probate act. The benefit of keeping the issues in the Probate Division is that the judges are more familiar with the related issues and they are more flexible on the procedure and willing to commit to closure in a timely manner on the various issues since the goal is to administrate in a diligent manner to close an estate.

Developing a Probate Strategy: Managing Client Expectations

The most important aspect of developing a probate administration strategy is to listen to the client and figure out exactly what their goals and objectives are. The client generally has an idea of what the means to the end should be—although in most cases, they will find out that is not how the process works. Therefore, it is important to inform the client exactly what is entailed in the probate process and explain the timeline, especially when litigation is involved—and that means that you need to be able to correctly manage your client's expectations and patience. Failure to do so will inevitably result in a dissatisfied client, because the process always takes longer than they think it should. Consequently, it is important to walk the client through the process as much as possible—for example, there are notice provisions in the statute that must be complied with and these can easily be set out for the client as you discuss the timeline. You typically need to lower their expectations as far as timing is concerned, and explain in detail what they can expect to happen given their objective and the potential conflicting objectives of the other parties involved.

The first step in developing a successful probate strategy is narrowing down the issues with the client, because the issues involved are often very emotional and personal and may require a lot of hand-holding. Next, you need to come up with a plan that makes the client feel comfortable, and explain the procedure involved so that they can understand the process. I have found that this early stage planning tends to eliminate the constant inquiries, which will reduce the cost to the estate, as well as any resulting irritation experienced and disclosed by the client, however irrational it may be. Essentially, I try to set a probate strategy road map at the outset to provide the client with confidence that they are in good hands and that their objectives are my priority, which gives the client peace of mind.

If the client expresses concern at the length of time that any given matter is taking, I often like to bring the client to court so that they can experience firsthand how the process works. I can explain to the client that motion practice is timely, that extensions may be given, and that the actual hearing may not occur until after a lengthy status date is set, but until the client actually sees the attorneys and the judge discussing and handling the matter, while they still may be frustrated, it is now a managed frustration. The client's fascination that the judge is favoring the other attorney or party, or that there is something going on, can be quickly dismissed by letting the client take part.

Common Arguments in Trust Litigation

Will and trust construction disputes are one of the most common forms of estate litigation. While there is no singular issue that can cover all cases, a typical argument relates to the definition of the terms within the documents. When it comes to term definition and interpretation, there is a 5th District Court of Appeals case that sets forth a good strategy to argue a construction case. See *Timmons v. Ingraham*, 36 So.3d 861 (Fla. 5th DCA 2010). This case involved the attempted disinheritance of the children by the stepmother.

Another common argument involves undue influence over the decedent by a beneficiary of the will or trust. The typical scenario involves a sibling who is entitled to receive a greater share of the estate assets than the other siblings are. The alleged reason for the inequity in the distribution is because the "favored" sibling exerted control over the parent and his or her assets prior to death while mom or dad was ailing. The favored sibling usually is the one who took care of the parent during their advanced age and handled most if not all of their finances. In doing so, favored child endeared her or himself to the parent and through a strategy of convincing the parent they needed to handle all aspects of their life, created a fiduciary relationship in which the parent was completely reliant upon favored child. The favored child most likely, depending upon independence of the parent, contacted the attorney to arrange for the preparation of new estate planning documents or amendments to the existing documents, which now increases the share of the favored sibling. Regardless of the reasoning, the good faith or the validity of this action, the other siblings have standing to litigate the issue and the mere fact that favored sibling contacted attorney, despite being at the direction of the parent. Taking the parent to the attorney while they discuss the changes to the documents is looked down upon by the courts and could result in the undoing of the parent's wishes. The caregiver child should be careful not to use his or her own attorney, should not be present during the discussions, and should not have any meaningful dialogue with the attorney regarding the terms of the will or trust. If this is the case, then the caregiver child may use the attorney as a witness to rebut sibling claims.

The Impact of Jurisdiction

Jurisdiction plays a huge role when you are dealing with probate cases. Usually you see the same lawyers all of the time so you know the key players and personalities involved in any given case. Probate court has somewhat of a small town mentality in that the same attorneys are there all the time; consequently, they can work closely with the judges and have some influence on how the process is going to work—depending upon their reputation, of course.

I have practiced in a couple of different probate jurisdictions, and they all seem to have that same small town mentality, for lack of a better term, but each operates very differently. Over time, you come to understand the personalities of the judges that you work with on a regular basis, and that is going to dictate how you craft your strategy when making a case before a given judge within a given jurisdiction. Some judges are stricter on how they apply procedure and others are very flexible. Ultimately, the personalities of the judges and attorneys in these cases have a lot to do with how things move forward in the probate process.

Key Issues in a Complicated Trust and Probate Case

When you first meet with a trust and probate client and listen to their story, you need to start probing and asking a number of questions. There are certain details that the client may not know are important; therefore, you need to figure out exactly what they key facts are, the personalities of the parties involved, the objectives of each of the conflicting parties, and what proofs are available. The emphasis is on what proofs are available. Do not waste your time or your client's money without confirming that you have a trail of documents or testimony to rely upon.

It is critical to read all of the estate planning documents involved, confirm the existence of prior documents, and review them all to see the story from the decedent's perspective. Ultimately, that is all that matters, if it is available. Don't throw anything away. A claim involving undue influence, for example, is a complicated and difficult case to prove. Therefore, you will need to see any doctor reports regarding the health history of the deceased parent/testator and documents relating to how they handled their finances. Proofs related to familial relationships, including letters or cards, may also be relevant. You will need to provide ample evidence to the court of the story you are trying to portray. Just because a client thinks something happened a certain way will not suffice. If a client senses during the life of the parent/testator an issue will arise, don't wait to take action in order to maintain the integrity of the documentation. Record keeping to preserve the "story" will be key to a successful litigation.

Managing Documents and Filings

Our firm has a docket department as well as a file department. Each case has its own file, and within that file are sub-files. Each attorney has their own assistant to make sure all the files contain the proper documents and that they are in order. We also have a computer database where documents and e-mails related to a case are saved under the client number. Pleadings and other documents received from other parties can be easily scanned and saved into this system under the client number. This system provides us with an efficient method of managing any given case and retrieving documents easily. The efficiency benefits the client and reduces the risk that with multiple attorneys reviewing a file or needing access to documents, that such documents will be unavailable when you need them.

Helpful Resources and Innovative Strategies

Unfortunately, there is not a lot of new case law in the probate area, as previously noted, although there are some secondary research sources such as *Bogert's Handbook on Trusts* that you can use for general ideas. If you are lucky you will find a case that you can use to assist in developing your strategy, but typically, you will find that in probate. The Probate Act itself along with the Probate ICLE provides the tools and good insight as to various techniques to assist in proceeding with any probate administration. I always recommend looking at the statutes first before proceeding—the answer just may be that easy.

Among the most innovative techniques that have been implemented by attorneys to handle some of the issues that are arising in this area is the use of a citation instead of filing a lawsuit in another division in order to streamline the process of getting assets back into an estate when they have been converted by another party or the refusal to turn the assets over to the administrator to have them properly administered, along with resolving issues related to asset ownership. When noncompliance by a party related to the handling of estate assets is involved, instead of the frustrating practice of trying to convince parties to act properly through letters and phone calls to no avail, action seems to occur quickly when the unreasonable party is forced to explain their actions to the court. The citation itself is much easier to draft compared to a complaint so the inertia to overcome the cost to draft and file the complaint is circumvented by simply filing a citation in the probate estate.

Amending heirships can be complicated, and it would be nice if there were a better process and/or some innovations for establishing the heirs in a probate administration. At one time in Cook County the approval of using a genealogist to research the family tree came easily. Now this is frowned upon for some reason, so a similar technique would be helpful to assist in this process when complicated heirships spanning the far reaches of the globe are involved.

Preparing the Estate Planning Documents

In the scope of an undue influence case, the drafting attorney may be able to get a sense of the family dynamics by simply meeting with the family members involved and determining who appears to be calling the shots. It is critical to discuss the client's estate planning objectives outside the presence of any other family member, especially the family member who stands to inherit a greater share. Ask direct and specific questions to the client as to what their wishes are and the intent behind their wishes in order to make sure that no undue influence is involved. The drafting attorney will inevitably be called upon to testify regarding the events that took place in relation to the document preparation. It is critical to maintain good records of the conversations that took place throughout the process. The reputation of the drafting attorney may be at stake; therefore, the fee to prepare an estate plan in which the drafting attorney is not comfortable is not worth the criticism that will inevitably come.

Another best practice to protect the client's interests is to recommend that the client's documents be prepared by an attorney who specializes in estate planning. Unfortunately, unnecessary litigation is often created simply because clients mistakenly have a general practitioner prepare their estate planning documents. A standard form is insufficient and an attorney who does not specialize in this area may not understand all of the nuances required to prepare an effective and proper plan to satisfy the needs of any given client, which vary widely.

Complex Issues in the Trust and Probate Area

There are many complex issues that arise in the context of the trust and probate area, including tax issues, construction issues, and the determination of the general intent of the testator. Other claims that drive litigation don't relate to the construction of the documents but rather the implementation of the administration of the documents by the executor/administrator/trustee. With litigation inevitably comes the destruction of familial harmony.

I have recently been involved in a complex probate case involving a four-year-old estate that includes a family-owned business, which encompasses the crux of the issues. By way of background, two friends decided to start a business together. They trusted that in the event that one partner was to die or become disabled, the other partner would take care of him and/or his family. So they were never concerned with putting any documentation in place to handle the succession of the business. One partner dies leaving a second wife and children from his first marriage. Not surprisingly, the surviving partner has no interest in giving up any portion of the business for the benefit of the family members. Nor does he feel he has any requirement to do so. The executor who was appointed in the probate estate is the son of the decedent. Sadly, the attorneys for the executor have misguided the executor on how to handle the proceedings relative to handling the valuation and buyout of the decedent's interest in the business. Additionally, the son has his own ideas on how things should be handled. Not surprising, the surviving second wife, who has been cut out of the process by the children and the attorneys, and has been denied information regarding the process and who is also frustrated that the process seems to be stalled with no action being taken to the detriment of the estate during the last four years, has now been forced to retain counsel and take efforts to remove the son as executor for his failure to comply with his duties. Familial harmony has been destroyed, the estate assets have been depleted by attorneys' fees because of the useless actions taken, and the business that was once thriving has become devalued by the current market conditions and possible manipulation by the surviving partner. Had the partners simply paid the relatively nominal attorneys' fees to put the proper documents in place to protect their interests and provide direction upon the death of a partner, this all could have been avoided saving the family and the estate. With respect to any succession planning, business owners need to consult with key advisors (such as an accountant, attorney, appraiser, financial advisor, and insurance agent) in order to preserve their life's work, provide continuity within the business, ensure financial security for the family, and preserve familial relationships. Failure to do so is a recipe for disaster.

Looking to the Future

Currently, we are in a state of flux and operating in an estate tax limbo. The federal estate tax is gone for a year, and it will probably be coming back soon, although no one can say exactly when or what it will look like. The estate tax repeal affects very few people. In 2009, less than one percent of the population needed to be concerned about estate taxes. But regardless of your net worth, you still need an estate plan because estate planning goes far beyond taxes.

Consider giving your estate plan a checkup. Be sure you have all the basic estate planning documents in place to leave your assets to the people or charities that you wish to benefit. If you fail to have the proper documents in place, the government will dictate where your assets will go. If you have minor children or children with special needs, name a guardian and leave funds for them in good hands in case something happens to you. If you fail to do this, the courts will appoint a guardian for you, which may be in complete contradiction to your wishes.

Unfortunately, despite not having disposable income due to the economy to pay for an estate plan, you cannot afford the ramifications, financially and emotionally, of not having a plan in place. At the very least, if you have minor children, have a simple will prepared to set forth your wishes related to guardianship and the ultimate disposition of your assets. Without a trust you will not avoid probate to transfer the assets, but at the very least, you will provide your family and the courts with a road map of how you want your estate to be administered. Give yourself that peace of mind.

Final Thoughts

I believe that one of the most important elements of success in this area is to strive to maintain civility with other attorneys. Although litigation is personal to the client, it should never be personal for the attorney. The key is to always act with integrity, and in doing so, a good reputation as an attorney will follow. A good reputation will not only benefit yourself but your clients as well.

Because estate planning and probate deal with issues of such a personal nature, it is critical to be a good listener—to really listen to your client's concerns and needs, and to be compassionate in your response.

Key Takeaways

- The most important aspect of developing a probate litigation strategy is to listen to the client and figure out their objective. You need to be able to correctly manage your client's expectations and patience. If you do not do that, the client is never going to be happy, because the process always takes longer than they think it should.
- The first step in developing a successful probate strategy is narrowing down the issues with the client. Essentially, set a probate strategy road map at the outset to reflect the relevant issues and to make sure that the client has a sufficient understanding of the process in order to set expectations.

- Unfortunately, a lot of unnecessary litigation is created because estate planning documents are drafted by attorneys who do not specialize in this area. Consequently, I always recommend that clients talk to a specialist in the area, and only have their documents prepared by an estate planning attorney.
- When you first meet with a trust and probate client and listen to their story, be sure to ask a number of questions to understand the issues in the case and the objectives of the client. More importantly, review the decedent's estate planning documents to determine intent of the decedent and confirm the client understands the key terms in the documents and their obligations and rights as either the executor/trustee or beneficiary.

Colleen Chinlund is a partner in the Chicago office of Arnstein & Lehr LLP. Her practice is concentrated in the areas of estate planning and probate and trust administration. Ms. Chinlund provides comprehensive counseling to help clients protect, preserve, and devise a plan for a tax-efficient distribution of estate assets. Ms. Chinlund has substantial experience representing a broad range of individuals and institutions in connection with their estate planning and administration needs, as well as business succession planning for family-owned and other closely held businesses. A substantial portion of her practice is devoted to administering decedent estates and representing fiduciaries in estate and trust administration and litigation matters.

Assisting Clients with Challenges to Their Trust Litigation Strategies

Scott A. Harshman

Partner

Jeffer Mangels Butler & Mitchell LLP

ASPATORE

Recent Cases in Trust and Probate Litigation

The recent cases in trust and probate litigation vary; however, a trend is appearing in response to a volatile stock market. Investment decisions or a lack of affirmative action by trustees can lead to a significant decrease in the trust estate. Often these decisions are viewed in hindsight and second-guessed by beneficiaries, which leads to a common cause of action—breach of fiduciary duty under the Uniform Prudent Investor Act (UPIA). Almost all states have adopted the UPIA, which is generally a set of standards that govern how a trustee invests the trust estate. These standards include the duty to monitor, investigate, and prudently manage the assets of the trust estate. The UPIA allows the settlor of the trust to modify, amend, or waive its provisions, but many settlors opt to include the entire UPIA, or if the trust is silent on whether it applies, the UPIA will apply by state statute.

In *Merrill Lynch Trust Company, FSB v. Campbell*, No. 1803-VCN, 2010 WL 1366992 (Del. Ch. March 31, 2010), Merrill Lynch Trust Company, FSB (Merrill) served as trustee of a charitable remainder annuity trust, an irrevocable trust. This type of trust by its very nature involves competing interests by the beneficiaries, because there is an income beneficiary, usually the settlor of the trust, and a remainder beneficiary, which is a charitable entity. While the income beneficiary seeks to maintain the annual payout for his or her lifetime, the remainder beneficiaries' interests are to maximize the growth of the trust assets. To achieve the goals of the trust, Merrill invested the trust corpus in all equity securities. Based upon advice from the settlor's outside investment advisor, in the year 2000, Merrill as trustee increased the risk in the portfolio in order to meet the income needs of the settlor. This was obviously an ill-timed decision, as the stock market decreased substantially after September 11, 2001.

At the heart of the claims made by Campbell was a breach of fiduciary duty by Merrill based upon the UPIA. The court noted that "MTLC faced something of a fiduciary 'Morton's Fork' when charged with the Trust's management: either take large risks in an attempt to satisfy its duties to all beneficiaries and fulfill the terms of the Trust Agreement, or concede from the very beginning that the Trust would fail; choosing instead to manage its assets by seeking goals other than those found in the Trust Agreement." The UPIA requires that the trustee invest the trust assets as a prudent investor, in light of the purposes, terms, distribution requirements, and other circumstances of the trust, and to diversify the investments of the overall portfolio unless it is prudent not to do so. A trustee will not be held liable to a beneficiary to the extent the trustee acted reasonably on reliance of the trust terms, and the liability of the trustee is not to be determined based on hindsight or subsequently developed facts and circumstances. The Court held that based on the competing mandates of the beneficiaries, the decision to invest highly in equities was reasonable. The Court further held that Merrill did not breach its fiduciary obligations under the UPIA. The terms of the trust, and the high distribution payout mandated by the trust in particular, tied Merrill's hands, and Merrill chose a course of investment strategy that was most likely to result in satisfaction of the trust's terms. The Court went on to state that "MLTC, however, cannot be held liable for failing to anticipate the precipitous drop in the market, and it cannot be held liable merely because market forces have proven that its investment decisions were poor ones."

It is clear from this case that obtaining a factual record that shows the analysis of the trustees' investment decisions is extremely important. The trustee must be able to prove that it acted reasonably, as a prudent investor, on each investment decision unless, as is shown in this case, the trust terms mandate a different approach or modify this standard. In either case, documenting the facts and analysis will go a long way in proving whether a trustee acted reasonably. A lack of evidence as to investment strategy and analysis may prove that a trustee acted imprudently.

Another important point made in this case is that the investment decisions must be reviewed in light of all the circumstances at the time the decision is made; hindsight or facts that occur later are not to be considered.

Finally, in preparing for litigation on a breach of trust under the UPIA, the litigator must take into account the terms of the trust and its distribution requirements. Although it may appear at first that a trustee acted imprudently under the standards of the UPIA, the trust instrument itself often mandates a different approach by the trustee. Here, Merrill's action to invest 90 percent of the portfolio in equities appears at first blush to patently violate the duty to diversify the trust's assets; however, this investment strategy was held reasonable in light of the trust terms.

In a recent Virginia case, *Karo v. Wachovia Bank*, No. 3:09CV575-HEH, 2010 WL 1930118 (E.D.Va. May 12, 2010), a beneficiary of the trust alleged breach of fiduciary duty by the trustee for failing to diversify the trust portfolio of assets and breach of the duty of loyalty because Wachovia failed to assume control of the trust from the other co-trustee. Wachovia Bank was appointed as co-trustee with another individual, Tony Karo, who was also a beneficiary of the trust. This is a common trustee structure where a bank acts as co-trustee with an individual beneficiary. The trust held Wachovia stock amounting to 65 percent of the trust estate. The trust instrument had specific language that allowed the trustee to retain the assets originally transferred into the trust and allowed the trustee broad discretion in making investments. The trust provided that the trustees could "invest the trust property and from time to time alter, change, or vary such investments and reinvestments thereof without being confined to investments lawful through the state or otherwise for fiduciaries under Virginia law." Although the court held that the language in the trust did not grant an unlimited waiver of the prudent investor rule, the language did specifically waive the prudent investor rule as to the Wachovia stock transferred into the trust. The plaintiff also made the argument that Wachovia should have unilaterally sold the Wachovia stock, but the court noted that the trust required unanimous consent by the co-trustees, and therefore, "as long as Tony withheld consent, Wachovia was powerless to act. Consequently this contention cannot support a beach of prudence claim."

On the second cause of action regarding breach of the duty of loyalty, the plaintiff made an interesting argument. The plaintiff alleged that Wachovia should have taken control of the trust by attempting to remove the individual co-trustee because Tony was an "unavailable" co-trustee. Tony Karo was provided with retention letters from Wachovia that explained that the trust had a concentrated stock position and Tony affirmed in writing that he desired to retain this concentrated position, and Tony executed a durable power of attorney to Drew Karo, his son, who was often making decisions on behalf of Tony Karo. It is somewhat unclear from the case why Drew stepped in to make these decisions, but there was some discussion in the case about whether Tony had mental capacity. The court ultimately held that there was no breach of loyalty by Wachovia because Tony was in fact participating in decisions for the trust by signing the retention letters and participating in governing the trust.

An important trust litigation avoidance strategy can be learned from this case. In drafting trust language that modifies the prudent investor rule, the attorney must be knowledgeable of the state's laws (i.e., has the state adopted the Uniform Prudent Investor Act, or some version of it) and draft any modification of the law so that it is unambiguous as to which portions are being modified and to which assets the modification applies. Had the language in the Karo trust been clearer in referring to the specific section of the prudent investor rule being waived and that the waiver specifically applied to the Wachovia stock, it is possible that the claim based on breach of duty under the prudent investor rule could have been avoided.

A possible emerging area of fiduciary liability has occurred with Irrevocable Life Insurance Trusts (ILIT). The typical structure of the ILIT is that the trust holds a single asset or asset class that is a life insurance policy. Specifically, a trustee's failure to periodically review the performance of the life insurance policy itself and the investments inside the policy may lead to a potential breach of fiduciary duty by the trustee.

The case of *In Re Matter of the Stuart Cochran Irrevocable Trust v. KeyBank, N.A.*, 901 N.E.2d 1128 (Ct. App. Indiana, 2009), demonstrates the potential for trustee liability for trust owned life insurance policies and the steps taken by the trustee to avoid such liability. The Court framed the issue by stating that "in essence, based on the circumstances facing the Trust in 2003, was it prudent for the Trustee to move the trust assets from insurance policies with significant risk and likelihood of ultimate lapse into an insurance policy with a smaller but guaranteed death benefit?" Again, this case involved an action due to a downturn in the stock market. When it was clear to the trustee that the investments inside the policy had substantially decreased so that the policy could no longer support the cost of insurance, the trustee retained an independent insurance consultant to review the situation. This type of policy is commonly known as a VUL, or variable universal life policy. These policies have underlying investments, and after September 11, 2001, when the stock market was in a severe decline, the investments lost value and the income generated by these investments could no longer support the costs of the policy. After receiving advice from the insurance consultant, KeyBank exchanged the VUL policies for one policy that was whole, guaranteed for the life expectancy of the insured, but that had a much lower death benefit.

The Court held that the trustee acted prudently and did not breach its fiduciary duty under the UPIA. The Court stated that KeyBank acted in a way that was "eminently prudent, reduction in death benefit notwithstanding" because it was faced with "(1) a rapidly declining stock market; (2) the most recent two years, in which the Trust had lost progressively more money, with every reason to believe that further erosion would occur with every day it held the VUL policies; (3) a grantor in his early fifties with a life expectancy of eighty-eight years; (4) a grantor who has lost a great deal of money because of the economic decline and, consequently, had no further funds to invest in the trust; and (5) a trust that consisted of two life insurance policies that an independent expert estimated could lapse within approximately five years if no further funds were invested."

In a declining stock market, trustees must be exceptionally diligent, because although the UPIA provides that hindsight and later facts and circumstances cannot be used as evidence of a breach of fiduciary duty, once the market begins to decline due to market trends, the trustee must take action to preserve trust property and invest at that time as a prudent investor would. A collateral claim in this case made by the beneficiaries was the lack of accounting and information provided by the trustee on an annual basis. The Court noted that timely financial reports would not have changed the negative financial condition of the trust and that "financial trends outside of the control of the Trustee or the Beneficiaries were the direct and proximate cause of the problem facing the Trust in 2003."

Although a life insurance policy is a special asset, the UPIA does apply to trustees of ILITs, unless the trust instrument modifies the UPIA. These duties include monitoring the policy performance and the investments inside the policy, investigating the suitability of the policy and its investments, and managing the policies as a prudent investor. Most notably in this case, the trustee obtained an independent review of the policies by an expert consultant. The Court gave this fact substantial weight in relieving the trustee of liability, and a trustee should strongly consider periodically hiring a consultant to review the policy.

Although the beneficiaries were unsuccessful in this case, they nonetheless litigated this matter completely based on a severe decrease in market conditions. As asset values decrease and trust estate are depleted, a corporate or bank trustee is often a prime target to recover losses. As markets continue to trend downward or are volatile, this appears to greatly increase the likelihood of litigation. When assets are growing in value year after year, the litigation trend decreases, and potential breaches of fiduciary duties are often overlooked by the beneficiaries. Once the trust has lost substantial value, then the trustee's actions are put under a microscope by the beneficiaries who are looking for ways to recover assets.

Another area of concern for any litigation matter or settlement is making the court action or settlement agreement enforceable against unknown, unborn, minor or incapacitated, or contingent beneficiaries. Since trusts and estates often have beneficiaries that cannot represent themselves in the current litigation matter, the issue always arises as to how to protect their interests. Many states have dealt with this issue by adopting the Uniform Trust Code, or some form of it, or alternatively case law has developed to provide that these beneficiaries may be virtually represented. Section 304 of the Uniform Trust Code provides that "Unless otherwise represented, a minor, incapacitated, or unborn individual, or a person whose identity or location is unknown and not reasonably ascertainable, may be represented by and bound by another having a substantially identical interest with respect to the particular question or dispute, but only to the extent there is no conflict of interest between the representative and the person represented." In a recent case in North Carolina, *First Charter Bank v. American Children's Home*, 692 S.E.2d 457 (N.C. App. 2010), the court held that an estate of one decedent virtually represented the estates of three other decedent's estates because the four estates were to share equally in the assets being distributed to them. Since the four estates were to share equally, the court determined that their interests were substantially identical. Note the two important requirements of virtual representation: there must be a substantially identical interest and there must be no conflict of interest. Although trust and probate litigation disputes are often settled out of court, whenever there is an issue with interests of persons that cannot represent themselves, it is usually always a prudent course of action to have the settlement agreement approved by a court, and if necessary, obtain declaratory relief on the issue of virtual representation so that a court can ascertain whether the interests are substantially identical and that there is no conflict of interest. The parties would never want to enter into an agreement that they believe is binding, and then later find out that future heirs or beneficiaries are able to unwind the entire agreement because their interests were not represented. It is common practice for trust and probate litigators to have the court appoint a guardian ad litem to represent the interests of individuals in court proceedings. A guardian ad litem is usually a court appointed attorney whose sole responsibility is to protect the interests of minors and contingent beneficiaries in court proceedings.

Common Settlement Structures for Trust and Probate Litigation and Negotiation

Settlement structures in trust and probate litigation are very much dependent on the facts of the case. However, the parties to the settlement should always seek to resolve all issues in the agreement and to obtain the necessary waivers and releases, and above all, the settlement agreement must be enforceable. Prior to negotiations, it is often a good idea to obtain a tolling agreement, or an agreement that preserves the rights of the parties and tolls any applicable statute of limitations so that the parties can negotiate the terms of the settlement without fear of losing valuable rights.

The issues negotiated in the settlement are very fact specific; however, the settlement process is difficult in trust and probate litigation because there may often be significant sentimental or emotional issues that can lead to irrational parties. For example, when through settlement negotiations, one family member learns sensitive information about their deceased parent that was known to other family members during the parent's life, or when a deceased parent gave oral instructions to one family member to the exclusion of others, this can cause heated negotiations and reduce the chances of success for the settlement. This occurs often in the context of a family business. The parent who runs the family business may have several children that work in the business, but there is one child who has stepped up and taken a leadership role. The parent tells the child that because he has taken a leadership role, he promises to give the child the business, but does not tell the other child who works in the business his plan. When the parent dies without a will or trust, the children are left to negotiate a settlement regarding the business, or litigate the matter. The emotional issues involved in this situation are not simply financial; one child now learns that his parent favored the other child, which can be a strong impediment to the settlement process.

Strategic Components of Trust and Probate Litigation

The strategic components of trust and probate litigation are complex because the subject matter of the litigation can often involve the intersection between trust and probate law, family law, real property law, and income, estate, and generation skipping tax law. Each component of the litigation must be individually analyzed, and the position taken in the litigation must not substantially adversely affect the other components, if possible. In one trust and probate matter, there might be issues that involve beneficiaries and heirs rights; the rights of spouses such as community verses separate property; the income tax effects of various types of property; and the potential estate and generation skipping tax that can apply to potential transferees and beneficiaries. In addition, there may be punitive provisions (e.g., no contest clauses) in the operative documents that drastically affect certain beneficiaries based upon the positions that are taken in the litigation. The type and location of assets held in the trust or estate may also heavily play into the decisions that are made in the litigation. For example, if the estate or trust is illiquid, the rights of third parties such as creditors and taxing authorities often compel the litigation to take a different course. Assets held in different states may present various issues involving jurisdiction of the court over the property and the persons involved in the litigation.

Although each trust and probate litigated matter is unique, the strategic components of the litigation generally are (1) obtaining all the facts relating to the litigated matter, (2) analyzing each individual claim and the effect of each claim on the client's rights as a trustee, personal representative, beneficiary, or heir, (3) procedural, jurisdiction, and venue analysis, (4) potential defenses and bars to claims, and (5) the tax consequences, if any, to the claimant.

Changing Trends in Trust and Probate Litigation

As more and more trusts have been created over the years, this has naturally led to an increase in litigation. Trusts with smaller trust estates (i.e., under $10 million of assets) can often have a nonprofessional individual acting as trustee. This individual may be a family member, trust advisor, or business partner of the settlor of the trust. These individual trustees may have very little knowledge of trust law and are unaware of the potential liability they are incurring by accepting the trusteeship. These individual trustees may also sometimes try to administer the trust without advice from a lawyer or accountant, which can often lead to disastrous results.

The nonprofessional, individual trustee often has very good intentions, but each decision they make can be scrutinized and may eventually lead to litigation. The matter usually begins with a petition by a beneficiary to compel an accounting. When the accounting is received by the beneficiary, this may lead to further questions about the trustee's actions, including management of investments, distributions to beneficiaries and the duty of impartiality among beneficiaries, and the potential for a variety of breach of fiduciary duty claims.

One important changing trend in trust litigation is the potential for an elder abuse claim in addition to breach of trust. Elder abuse law allows an interested person to take action against individuals or facilities that abuse elderly persons. These claims are often made against skilled nursing facilities, residential care facilities, relatives of an elderly person, agents under a durable power of attorney, or conservators acting under a conservatorship. Although this is not trust or probate law, it is a quickly expanding area of litigation that often accompanies probate and trust litigation. Some elder abuse law provides for postmortem compensatory damages for pain and suffering (See California Welfare and Institutions Code § 15657.5).

Motivations of Claimants in Trust and Probate Litigation

The motivation of the claimant in trust and probate litigation usually stems from a perceived wrongdoing by the trustee or personal representative, or in the case of challenges against the drafting of the documents themselves, the motivation can often be an heir's understanding of his or her inheritance that differs from the dispositive provisions in the testamentary documents. This latter motivation can often lead to a claim of incapacity, undue influence, or mistake. These are the traditional claims that have occurred in trust and probate litigation. However, as explained earlier, the claims that are emerging now often deal with management of assets primarily caused by market factors, decreasing values in real estate, and the stock market.

Whereas a claim based on capacity of the testator or undue influence of the testator relies heavily on the facts surrounding the drafting, contacts, and communications with the testator by his or her attorney or others, the execution of the documents, and the medical records of the testator at the time of execution, the claims based on mismanagement of investments and breach of fiduciary duty under the UPIA rely heavily on expert testimony that the trustee or personal representative acted reasonably and prudently. Claims attacking the testamentary documents are heavily weighted on circumstantial evidence and the testimony of the drafting attorney, which is given substantial weight, but evidence to support claims based on management decisions of assets rely heavily on reviewing the trustee/personal representative's actions and analysis of the situation, the language in the will or trust that mandates an investment policy or distribution scheme, and the actions of the trustee/personal representative in preserving trust/estate property.

Protecting Trusts against Potential Litigation

The idea that a client would go to the trouble and expense to create a trust only to have it be the subject matter of later litigation is abhorrent to most clients. Therefore, the client should engage a reputable attorney who is an expert in will and trust law. Litigation is often the product of poorly drafted trust documents that provide for vague or unworkable provisions. The case discussed above, *Merrill Lynch v. Campbell*, is an example of a trust that as drafted was doomed to fail.

The client should insert a no-contest provision into the trust to create a disincentive for beneficiaries to contest its provisions. If the beneficiary has something to lose, then the thought of litigating the trust provisions is much less desirable. Trustee selection is a key component to avoiding trust litigation. The client should carefully consider all the options in choosing a trustee or co-trustees, and choose the individual or institution that will be diligent and experienced to follow the terms of the trust and administer the trust properly, hire experts to advise the trustee, and delegate trust management when appropriate.

Such defensive measures should always be pursued, because trust litigation is often unforeseen and can occur years later from when the trust document is created. However, there may be red flags that indicate potential litigation. Some of the factors to consider are the personalities of beneficiaries, the relationships of the beneficiaries to the settlor of the trust and to one another, persons who are natural heirs of the settlor who are disinherited in the trust document, and mental illness or capacity issues of the settlor.

The estate lawyer can help the client adopt these precautionary measures by having a frank and full discussion with the client about their family tree, asking questions about the relationships of the entire family, and asking direct questions about family dysfunction and what potential issues the client can foresee. An important precautionary measure is informing beneficiaries of the terms of the trust prior to the death of the settlor, which may be best done through a family meeting. The settlor can then affirm his or her testamentary intent and potentially avoid later litigated matters dealing with incapacity, undue influence, and mistake.

The capacity of the settlor of a trust is a common litigated issue. The standards for mental capacity can vary from state to state, but generally, a person does not have mental capacity to execute testamentary documents if either of the following is true:

(1) The individual does not have sufficient mental capacity to be able to (A) understand the nature of the testamentary act, (B) understand and recollect the nature and situation of the individual's property, or (C) remember and understand the individual's relations to living descendants, spouse, and parents, and those whose interests are affected by the will.

(2) The individual suffers from a mental disorder with symptoms including delusions or hallucinations, which delusions or hallucinations result in the individual's devising property in a way which, except for the existence of the delusions or hallucinations, the individual would not have done. (See California Probate Code § 6100.5).

One important aspect of mental capacity is that it is judged at the time when the testamentary documents are executed. It is possible for a person to have capacity one day and then to lack capacity the next day. In addition, note that at least in California, even though the settlor may suffer from a mental disorder, the settlor must devise his or her property in a way that he or she otherwise would not have done if there was capacity. Therefore, it is not enough to simply prove that a person has hallucinations, delusions, dementia, Alzheimer's disease, etc., at the time of executing testamentary documents, which often can be done by obtaining the person's medical records through the discovery process. To prove that a settlor would have created a different estate plan had he not had a mental disorder can be difficult. This is somewhat like proving a negative, or the absence of something. However, if after a person suffers from a mental disorder, they significantly change the provisions of the trust and such changes are inconsistent with the person's expressed desires to others, then there may be good cause to believe that but for the mental disorder, the person would not have changed their trust.

Just prior to the signing of testamentary documents, the attorney should have the client affirm certain important facts regarding the execution of the documents. This "document execution checklist" provides a contemporaneous affirmation of intent and mental capacity that can later be used to defend the estate plan. The execution document should ask the client executing the documents the following important questions: (1) Have you examined and do you approve of these documents? (2) Do these documents accurately reflect your wishes regarding the disposition of your property upon your death? (3) Do you have any questions about these documents? (4) Have you recently had any drug, alcohol or other substances that would influence your thought processes? (5) Has anyone placed any pressure, duress or other influence upon you regarding any of these documents? (6) Is this document intended to be your will/living trust? (7) Do you want us to witness your will? If there are any potential issues with the mental capacity of the person executing the estate plan, then it may be a prudent step to obtain the opinion of a medical doctor that the person does have the mental capacity to understand the documents and the execution of the documents. It may be a good idea to videotape the execution of testamentary documents so that it can later be used as evidence documenting the capacity of the settlor of the trust, but the lawyer suggesting this strategy must be careful that the settlor is comfortable with videotaping the execution of the documents and that the video does not inadvertently make the settlor appear to be incompetent. Instead of defending the estate plan, this videotape evidence can later be used to invalidate it.

Final Thoughts

It is important for an attorney in this area to undertake a thoughtful and careful analysis of each claim, considering all the ramifications of the claims. It is difficult for an attorney to be simultaneously an expert in trust and probate law, family law, real property law, and tax law; therefore, the best advice is that when a claim has an impact on these various facets of the law, a team approach is often best. It may be necessary to have the trust, probate and tax expert team up with the seasoned litigation attorney to develop a successful strategy for the client.

Key Takeaways

- In preparing for litigation on a breach of trust under the UPIA, the litigator must take into account the terms of the trust and its distribution requirements. Although it may appear at first that a trustee acted imprudently under the standards of the UPIA, the trust instrument itself often mandates a different approach by the trustee.
- In drafting trust language that modifies the prudent investor rule, the attorney must be knowledgeable of the state's laws (i.e., has the state adopted the Uniform Prudent Investor Act, or some version of it) and draft any modification of the law so that it is unambiguous as to which portions are being modified and to which assets the modification applies.
- Although trust and probate litigation disputes are often settled out of court, whenever there is an issue with interests of persons that cannot represent themselves, it is usually always a prudent course of action to have the settlement agreement approved by a court, and if necessary, obtain declaratory relief on the issue of virtual representation so that a court can ascertain whether the interests are substantially identical and that there is no conflict of interest.
- The estate lawyer can help the client adopt precautionary measures in relation to their trust by having a frank and full discussion with the client about their family tree, asking questions about the relationships of the entire family, and asking direct questions about family dysfunction and what potential issues the client can foresee. An important precautionary measure is informing beneficiaries of

the terms of the trust prior to the death of the settlor, which may be best done through a family meeting.

- Just prior to the signing of testamentary documents, the attorney should have the client affirm certain important facts regarding the execution of the documents. This "document execution checklist" provides a contemporaneous affirmation of intent and mental capacity that can later be used to defend the estate plan.
- It is difficult for an attorney to be simultaneously an expert in trust and probate law, family law, real property law, and tax law; therefore, the best advice is that when a claim has an impact on these various facets of the law, a team approach is often best. It may be necessary to have the trust, probate and tax expert team up with the seasoned litigation attorney to develop a successful strategy for the client.

Scott A. Harshman, a partner at Jeffer Mangels Butler & Mitchell LLP, has extensive experience in tax, trust and estate matters, including probate and trust litigation and administration, wealth transfer planning, income tax planning, corporate and partnership taxation, federal and state tax controversy, business succession planning, and charitable planning.

Mr. Harshman is a certified specialist in estate planning and trust and probate law by the State Bar of California Board of Legal Specialization. He is a member of the Trusts and Estates Section of the California State Bar.

Mr. Harshman is recognized as a "Southern California Rising Star" by Los Angeles Magazine *and* Super Lawyers Magazine, *2010. He is the author of many articles related to estate planning.*

Mr. Harshman received his LL.M. in taxation from the University of San Diego School of Law, his J.D., cum laude, from Whittier Law School and his B.A. from University of California, Riverside.

Key Factors Influencing Today's Trust and Probate Cases

Robert J. Selsor

Chairman, Fiduciary and Estate Litigation Practice Group

Polsinelli Shughart PC

ASPATORE

Key Trust and Probate Cases

I believe that the most powerful trend in the trust and probate area is not found with evolving case law, but rather through statutory enactments such as the Uniform Trust Code, which are expanding their reach throughout the country. The UTC is now the law in approximately half of the states and in a large sense represents a codification of the common law that existed before its enactment, as well as a synthesis of various state statutory frameworks. The Code, in much the same way as the UCC streamlined the law of business in an earlier day, provides much greater uniformity from state to state as well as resolution of conflicting case law. Its greatest contribution, however, is simply a clear, concise guide to the rules that govern trusts.

Case law is, of course, relevant as a citation of legal authority. But practitioners can learn a great deal from prior cases simply because they give insight into human nature and allow the lawyer reading them to focus on them from an entirely objective perspective. Objective reactions to particular sets of facts can be invaluable later when confronting a new set of facts for a current client. For example, the disinherited prodigal son may be viewed in one light by a neutral observer and in another by someone else, including sometimes the lawyer, with an emotional stake in the outcome.

Therefore, a lawyer's litigation strategy must blend an understanding of the realities of the law—claims, defenses, and elements of each—with the realities of how a case will be perceived. Choosing one strategy, for example, may allow different evidence to be presented to a judge or jury, or make the difference in having a judge or jury as fact finder in the first instance. For example, in a case involving a trust and a defendant's alleged manipulations of the grantor, it may make a great deal of sense to include small claims involving the trustee's use of a power of attorney for the same grantor to benefit himself. Even if the claims are for only a few hundred or a few thousand dollars, including the claim may increase the chances that evidence of the other conduct may be presented to the finder of fact in order to resolve those claims. Otherwise, introduction of such evidence may depend on the plaintiff's attorney establishing a pattern of conduct or habit on the part of the defendant that may require several additional examples of bad acts under applicable evidentiary doctrines. But showing the finder of fact that the defendant is an opportunist who has used his power to benefit himself in other areas can make the difference between winning and losing in a close case. The ability to assess claims for their later evidentiary value, in addition to the normal checklist of considerations, is the mark of a truly sophisticated litigator.

The Impact of the Economy and Demographics on Trust and Probate Litigation

The current economy seems to be having a dampening effect on some types of litigation where potential litigants, as in other areas of litigation, may not have the level of resources necessary to wage a war in the courts that they might have had five years ago. Estates are often smaller because of decreased asset values, meaning that some tax and statute-driven estate formulas yield different outcomes than would have been the case before portfolios and real estate values, among other things, decreased with the Great Recession. Sometimes this outcome will actually incentivize people to litigate and sometimes it will not. For example, a trust that first leaves assets equal to the estate tax exemption cutoff in a credit shelter or bypass subtrust, may leave fewer assets now to other subtrusts created for other heirs or loved ones including a spouse. Such an outcome may force a spouse to challenge this estate planning if, for example, he or she now is receiving a relatively small amount in a marital trust and has no income rights under the bypass or credit shelter trust. On the other hand, if an estate has decreased in size, in some instances there may not be enough money to fight over relative to the cost of the litigation.

Likewise, demographic trends have had a substantial impact on this practice in some areas. The main demographic in my mind is the fact that people are living longer, and thus experiencing greater degrees and incidences of dementia that put the validity of late-created estate planning documents at issue and increase the need and frequency for involuntary guardianships and conservatorships. I sense that there are more of these cases being filed now than before. These cases often focus on whether the grantor or testator had the requisite testamentary capacity to make the changes to a trust and/or will or whether the amended documents involve undue influence. A living but demented individual may fall pray to manipulation and the wasting of his or her assets, necessitating the appointment of a conservator to protect the ward or protectee's financial holdings. A guardian can be appointed to protect such person's physical safety and make sure that the ward receives adequate food, clothing, shelter, and medical care.

Settlement Structures for Trust and Probate Litigation

The primary settlement structure for trust and probate litigation is division of estate assets, often with a characterization of the payments made as being an inheritance and legal fees rather than tort damages, to lessen the chance of taxable consequences.

Usually the division of assets is immediate, as opposed to the situation where payments are made over time, since the assets are available. Mutual releases are, of course, a must since weary litigants will be highly motivated to make sure that further litigation and claims do not arise in the future out of the same or similar circumstances. A release bars further claims and literally "releases" opposing parties from further liability beyond the terms of their settlement. Sometimes provision has to be made for possible unforeseen tax consequences and later claims against an estate. Since I am a fiduciary litigator and not a tax specialist, I often will have a tax expert review a settlement before I sign off to make certain there is no hidden tax trap that would upend the parties' expectations. For example, let's assume that a grantor established an irrevocable trust and that trust is challenged. A settlement that moves a portion of the trust assets to a non-beneficiary, or reapportions the assets among beneficiaries, runs the risk of triggering hefty gift tax issues that might be avoided depending on how the settlement is structured. Another example would be a challenge by a widow to her husband's estate planning. A settlement paid to her out of a bypass or credit shelter trust will increase the widow's taxable estate. Often that is not an issue but if the widow had substantial assets to begin with and the settlement puts her over the unified credit, then her heirs or beneficiaries may be forced to pay out approximately half of her recovery in estate taxes when such an outcome might have otherwise been avoided.

Strategic Components of Trust and Probate Litigation

The first step in trust and probate litigation from the plaintiff's perspective is freezing the assets to make sure they are available at the conclusion of a successful outcome. A plaintiff pursuing a fiduciary action or challenging a trust or will may also seek to cut off the opponent from the estate's resources so as to hinder their ability to defend, absent separate resources from which to do so. Thus, a motion to appoint a trustee ad litem or special fiduciary may cut off access to estate funds and put pressure on an opponent to settle, or at least limit the number of issues to be litigated. From the defense perspective, of course, the opposite goal is desired. A trustee who can finance his or her defense with trust funds is in a much better position to endure the litigation than one who must use his or her own personal funds to do so.

As referenced above, I think that choosing legal theories with an eye toward considering what evidence each will allow you to introduce into evidence is also appropriate (e.g., bringing a claim for even small indulgences against a fiduciary or a beneficiary accused of undue influence may help the plaintiff to establish a pattern of misconduct that might not be otherwise achievable with a single focused claim).

Discovery is always important, whether on the plaintiff's side or the defense side. Many of these cases are proven or disproven with circumstantial evidence (since the grantor may be deceased), and thus it is even more important to seek out information from files, public records, and third party witnesses. Evidence tending to support or negate a trust grantor's view and opinions of a particular heir, for example, can be gleaned from interviews with close friends and acquaintances, correspondence, e-mails, and a host of other sources of information. Negative information about an opposing party, such as a prior criminal history or financial problems, may affect that party's credibility at trial. Medical records referencing a testator's confusion or diminished mental capacity may bolster a claim of undue influence or even a lack of testamentary capacity. Electronic discovery may reveal who the author of a document is or was and metadata may reveal prior versions of a document or other information tending to impact on its validity in some fashion in the context of a case where a particular document's validity is in question.

A thorough deposition of key parties is vitally important. Where capacity is at issue, the testimony of treating physicians can be critical and is often the most important factor in such a case. I also look to see if a de facto fiduciary or confidential relationship can be imposed on a defendant. Most states require several elements to be established as a precondition to establishing this type of relationship including that one person was "subservient to the dominant mind and will of the other," that there was a surrender of independence, trust between the parties, and several other requirements. See e.g., *Kratky v. Musil*, 969 S.W.2d 371, 377 n.1 (Mo. App. W.D. 1998). Establishment of such a relationship can allow for a claim of constructive fraud (fewer elements to prove than with common law fraud) and can establish presumptions against the defendant that may increase the burden of defense.

Developing a Litigation Strategy

In developing a trust or probate litigation strategy, I look at how much time has passed since key events have occurred to see if there are limitation problems, since the deadlines for taking legal action in this area are much shorter than in other areas of the law. For example, in many states, a claim against an estate must be made within six months of published notice that an estate has been opened or else the claim will be forever barred. Contrast this with a general five year statute of limitations typically found for many civil claims or even a ten year statute of limitations for claims on a written contract. I then generally look at standing—does my client, or the opposing client, have the legal right to bring the claim at issue? For example, if my client wants to challenge a trust amendment and restore a trust to its prior form, was he or she a beneficiary under the earlier version of the trust? If not, there may not be legal standing.

I then consider what claims are available; the burden of proof with each (e.g., a trust contest may be a clear and convincing standard as opposed to preponderance standard under local case law); and, as referenced above, what evidence will each claim allow me to bring into the case. Some situations give rise to presumptions against a fiduciary if he or she has benefitted from a particular transaction. Sometimes the argument can be made that the burden of proof is actually shifted to the fiduciary! An awareness of these issues and thorough research can be outcome determinative in close cases. Likewise, certain claims allow for an award of attorneys' fees, where there is a specific statute in place for such purpose. Other claims may be governed by the American Rule, which assumes each litigant will bear the cost of their own legal fees regardless of the outcome.

To the extent a forum can be chosen, I look to see if I have a choice of venue or judges. In my primary practice jurisdictions, for instance, I can seek a change of judge early in the case. If a jury is to be empanelled, some jurisdictions are better than others are. Simply put, a different jurisdiction can mean a different judge or a different jury pool. In addition, the cost of prosecution or defense can be increased or decreased depending on the venue if parties are forced to travel long distances or are forced to hire local counsel to assist their primary counsel with issues of local practice. Increased financial burdens on a party, of course, can lead to positive settlement pressure.

I also want to know if I will have subpoena power over key witnesses and documents. If the case is outside of my normal geographic practice area, is there a strong local firm available with experience and skill in the particular court in which I may be filing suit? In some jurisdictions, whether a local attorney is "connected" is also, unfortunately, a necessary consideration.

With the spread of the Uniform Trust Code, there are more opportunities for litigants to recover their legal fees if successful, and sometimes even if they are not successful. I look to see if there is legal authority to support such an award with respect to a particular claim or defense. See e.g. UTC § 1004. Since fiduciary issues involve a higher standard of conduct on the part of a fiduciary than those imposed by the marketplace, consideration of punitive damages may also be appropriate.

Venue and judge selection is important as well because the right decision on these issues can take away some of the "unknowns" that often are present in this type of litigation. I also believe that having alternative claims available (e.g., having a claim based upon a fiduciary duty or power of attorney statute, when the facts support it) to supplement a trust or will contest is wise in case problems develop with your main claim. For example, I had a case where a trustee used a power of attorney to hire an attorney at law to amend a trust for the trustee's benefit. My clients were disinherited. I tried the trust contest to the court and lost, the court finding that we had not proven our case to the higher "clear and convincing evidence" standard necessary to prevail in that type of action. But we also sued the trustee for improper use of the power of attorney, a claim governed by a preponderance standard. The jury awarded actual and punitive damages in excess of what the trust contest would have provided.

Arguments and Legal Standards for Trust Litigation

The arguments for trust litigation all derive from the facts, and thus will vary from case to case. I think whatever argument one develops in a particular case must be measured as objectively as possible—i.e., how will this judge or a jury in this jurisdiction react to these facts? Themes such as "greed" and "jealousy" are often readily comprehended by these fact finders if, again, the facts support them.

Development of facts that focus on the relationship between parties or a particular party and a grantor/testator are important. The quality of those relationships will often be in dispute, and a variety of possible scenarios will be readily imaginable by the finder of fact (e.g., loyal son versus worthless, spoiled child; faithful second spouse versus "gold digger," etc).

The legal standards in these cases can influence the strategy significantly. A clear and convincing standard of proof is more difficult than a preponderance standard. In many jurisdictions, the establishment of a fiduciary relationship gives rise to presumptions against the fiduciary that, in some circumstances, can even reverse the burden of proof. Such a difference can make all the difference.

Litigating a Complex Trust/Probate Case

The complexity of a trust/probate case can vary significantly depending on how many people are involved, the amount of money at issue, and a variety of other factors. The more parties, the more complex the dynamics, the closer the evidence on certain issues—all give rise to additional dimensions to a case. Usually this increases the burden on the plaintiff unless the defense is poorly represented, disjointed, or underfunded, in which case a sophisticated plaintiff's trial team can gain an advantage. But, for example, in a trust contest case it may be necessary to also bring a will contest if the will is drafted in such a way as to reconstitute the trust's terms if for any reason the trust is defeated. Many sophisticated estate planners write wills in that fashion. Likewise, if several trust amendments are at issue, a challenge to each may be necessary to get the trust back to the point where there are no issues as to its legitimacy. In large multi-beneficiary cases, keeping track of who benefits from the litigation and who does not can be a challenge in and of itself.

I believe that open discussion with at least another colleague in the area, including estate planners, is a good start in developing a litigation strategy. Issues and responses from the other side need to be anticipated. An outline of strategy is a good idea in some cases including a recitation of available evidence, possible sources of positive and negative evidence, and all of the other normal considerations for bringing or defending a case in a particular court or jurisdiction.

Also, explaining to the client up front the complexities of the case and the likely duration and expense is necessary at an early stage so that expectations will be appropriately shaped from the beginning. Drawing up a budget is also a good idea. Securing experts and preliminary opinions early on is also appropriate. For example, an early examination of medical records, if available, by a doctor or, if appropriate, a geriatric psychiatrist, may provide a good early understanding of some of the pressure points in a case. Gathering as much information as possible before even filing suit, such as witness statements and medical records, is also a good idea. Although clients may pressure the attorney to launch into a case on the cheap and deal with these issues later, the preferred approach is to have as much of the facts and law distilled at the beginning.

Managing Documents

I always try to keep the case primarily electronic and use an "eroom" to store pleadings, correspondence, and key documents. I use Adobe to highlight and annotate key documents. These documents can be easily transmitted to clients for review and education. I use a database in court for larger cases. Legal research and fact investigation are always important. To prepare for trial, I identify key exhibits and outline depositions that have been taken.

Emerging Practices for Today's Trust and Probate Litigation

Emerging practices in this area include more mediation and some arbitration. Mediation involves non-binding negotiation between the parties presided over by a neutral mediator selected by the parties or by the court. Such a process tends to foster better communication and provides a filter for some of the negative and emotional reactions that are a hallmark in this area. Arbitration is generally binding and involves submission of a claim to a private arbitrator for determination outside of a public courtroom. Most states have statutes that govern and promote arbitration which is often thought to be faster and usually more cost effective than formal litigation. There have also been more contingency fee agreements or hybrid fee agreements, since many litigants simply cannot afford protracted legal representation.

New technology makes a case move more efficiently and less expensively. It allows a smaller firm to compete against a larger firm as, for example, where extensive document review may be replaced by scanning of documents and optical character recognition searches that may filter out massive amounts of irrelevant information and ultimately yield key evidence in the case. There are also cost pressures that are driving some of these trends. Audio-visual presentations are becoming the norm and in many cases, the standard for an effective courtroom presentation.

Advantages of Innovative Defenses

Most innovation that benefits the plaintiff's case will similarly benefit the defense as well. Cost-saving measures will positively affect any party. The ability to recover and scan electronic data helps both parties.

We believe in utilizing a library of form pleadings, checklists for various types of litigation, reliable and informed expert witnesses, and the services of a good private investigator. For example, a private investigator often is less expensive than an attorney or paralegal and often more effective at getting a witness to reveal information than may be the case with a less seasoned junior associate. Utilization of form pleadings means that the attorney does not have to "reinvent the wheel" for a particular type of case and likewise avoids much of the background research that a practitioner who "dabbles" in this area might experience.

Recent Developments in Trust and Probate Litigation

Recent changes in trust and probate litigation include more mediation and arbitration, as previously noted, because of economic pressure to avoid traditional litigation and calls from various public and private sectors for alternatives to the traditional lawsuit model. There have also been changes and refinements in the law (e.g., passage of the Uniform Trust Code, etc.) which have often streamlined the process for bringing a claim to court. Other key changes include application of modern methods and procedures (e.g., electronic discovery) that have made it easier to do legal research, to review diverse public records from a computer terminal in a law office, and to simply analyze vast amounts of information in far less time than was the case a generation ago.

Although there have also been advances in medicine to deal with dementia, more dementia is affecting grantors and testators, who are living longer. This has led to more trust and will contests involving dementia, including contested conservatorships and suits involving fiduciaries and attorneys. Trustee removal cases continue to be fairly common as well where, for example, a trustee who has made poor decisions or failed to keep beneficiaries informed may face the scrutiny of a probate court as a result of those defalcations. General market swings give rise to more of these suits as beneficiaries often blame their trustee for resulting losses in value. Trustees who culpably engage in self-dealing, as has always been the case, are an easy target. But money continues to be the overriding issue in most trust and probate cases although vindication of long-simmering family disputes might well be a close second.

Protecting Trusts against Potential Litigation

In terrorem clauses in estate planning are one of the best ways to protect trusts against potential litigation, although not all states enforce them. These clauses provide, for example, that a beneficiary may forfeit an existing benefit under a trust or will if they seek to contest other provisions in the document. Such a provision thus creates risk for a potential litigant beyond the cost of litigation, especially if the existing bequest is substantial. From the point of view of the grantor/testator, leaving a questionable heir a smaller bequest, rather than completely disinheriting them, sometimes will quell their feelings to a degree and, as referenced above, gives them something to lose if they choose to litigate and do not prevail.

Although not always a practical option, clients should also be advised not to change their estate planning, if possible, late in life. It is important to create documentation of the client's wishes. The client should also take steps to make certain that they will be well cared for during old age. Use of a trust company is a good idea, in many instances, since such institutions often have safeguards and well-developed practices for managing client assets. If nothing else, they also have "deep pockets" if problems arise. That is not always the case when a grantor names her brother-in-law to the position.

For serious planning for an expected challenge, contest, or lawsuit, you should consider changing the place of administration of a trust to a state with more favorable law. For example, in Missouri it is easier to change the terms of a trust or to even terminate it after death than is the case in most states. A grantor wanting to increase the chances of solidifying his or her estate planning for the long term might want to establish the administration of his or her trust across the river in Illinois or in another state.

Final Thoughts

An aging population may bring many of the issues of aging loved ones into the lives of more people. Those experiences will help to shape the views of potential jurors. In general, of course, an aging population will give rise to more potential for struggles over family assets. The increase in the use of trusts also has an impact, since the standard for contesting such a document is often more burdensome.

In order to succeed in these cases, you must make sure you have not allowed any time deadlines to pass. That determination needs to be made at the earliest possible juncture. Research your case up front and make sure your pleadings are solid and your theories defensible. You should also start your discovery right away. I like to serve document requests on an opposing party with the petition or complaint so that the clock will begin to run immediately on the opposing party's deadline for responding.

Key Takeaways

- Case law is, of course, relevant for citing legal authority. But practitioners can learn a great deal from prior cases simply because they give insight into human nature and allow the lawyer reading them to focus on them from an entirely objective perspective.

- Discovery is always important, whether on the plaintiff's side or the defense side. Many of these cases are proven or disproven with circumstantial evidence (since the grantor may be deceased), and thus, it is even more important to seek out information from files, public records, and third party witnesses.
- Also, explaining to the client up front the complexities of the case and the likely duration and expense is necessary at an early stage so that expectations will be appropriately shaped from the beginning. Drawing up a budget is also a good idea. Securing experts and preliminary opinions early on is also appropriate.
- In order to succeed in these cases, you must make sure you have not blown any time deadlines. Research your case up front and make sure your pleadings are solid and your theories defensible. You should also start your discovery right away. I like to serve document requests on an opposing party with the petition or complaint.

Robert J. Selsor is chairman of the Fiduciary and Estate Litigation Practice Group at Polsnelli Shughart PC, a national law firm with offices from Phoenix to New York, with a concentration of lawyers in the Midwest. Mr. Selsor is a fellow in the American College of Trust and Estate Counsel and is a widely published author and lecturer. A former Fulbright Scholar, Mr. Selsor is a graduate of the University of Missouri School of Law. His practice is divided between plaintiff and defense work, and he is also active as a mediator and arbitrator in the trust and probate area.

Changing Issues and Motivations in Trust and Probate Cases

Timothy W. Ridley

Partner

Meagher & Geer PLLP

ASPATORE

Introduction

We are an eighty-one-year-old firm focused on litigation. Our original focus was on insurance defense cases, where we were hired by insurance companies to represent drivers that were involved in car accidents. In 1980, our firm, Meagher & Geer, started to grow and began diversifying its practices. We now have about eighty lawyers and offices in Minneapolis, Minnesota and Scottsdale, Arizona. We have a very comprehensive practice, including various practice areas.

Meagher & Geer remains a litigation firm, but not just on behalf of insurance companies; there is a general practice portion of the firm—my area—that does estate planning and probate and trust-related litigation, as well as corporate and real estate work. Therefore, we can best be described as a broad-based firm with a litigation focus.

When I started my practice at Meagher & Geer in 1985—I am now a twenty-five-year veteran—I was primarily involved in estate planning. I worked with referrals and corporate clients that had shareholders or employees that needed wills and trusts drafted. However, over the years, my practice has evolved to the point where about 25 percent of my work involves estate planning, while the other 75 percent is comprised of litigation, and going forward, I feel that it is likely to stay at that percentage. The litigation in the probate and trust estate area generally deals with whether there is a valid will—i.e., was the person of adequate capacity to prepare the will when they signed it, or were they unduly influenced by somebody else? Alternatively, was the estate owner's personal representative or executor acting in the appropriate capacity, or were they acting in a self-centered way, rather than for the benefit of all the beneficiaries? In the trust area, I have found that there is significantly less litigation about the validity of a trust—i.e., whether the person had the capacity to write the trust, or whether they were unduly influenced in the writing of the trust. Rather, we see more litigation regarding the administration of the trust, and whether the trustee is acting appropriately in their fiduciary capacity; in other words, if it is an individual trustee, are they self-serving? I recently litigated a case where the trustee (the son of the trust maker and the father of the beneficiaries) treated the assets as his own rather than for the benefit of his children, the beneficiaries of the trust.

Recent Case Law in the Trusts and Probate Area

We recently held our State Bar Association Probate and Trust Section annual conference, which is a two-day continuing legal education (CLE) program. One of the session topics was recent case law. Basically, the participants go through case law over the past year and discuss the important cases, both nationally and locally. About twenty cases were discussed during this session, which was ninety minutes long. Of those cases, sixteen were in other jurisdictions and four were Minnesota cases—two of which were mine. It should be noted that there is very little reported case law in this practice area. If you are ever required to research the annotations on the estate and trust statutes in Minnesota, you will find very little.

Over the last couple of years, I have handled several interesting cases in the estates and trusts area. One was a case where I represented the mother of the deceased. The son was about thirty years old and he committed suicide. He was never married, he had no children, and he did not have a will. Therefore, we had to look to the intestate statute to determine who was going to be the executor. In this case, the parents were the ones who had the highest priority, but the parents were divorced. I represented the mother, who filed a petition to get herself appointed as executor. However, on the day of the hearing the husband came into court with their other son, who was the brother of the deceased. Apparently, the night before the hearing they had discovered a will that said that the brother should be the executor.

Consequently, although we had anticipated that we were going to have a fight about who was going to be the executor—the mother, the father, or a third person—it turned into a situation where the brother might be appointed as personal representative, because of the recently discovered will. As a result, we wound up going to trial on the issue of whether or not the will was valid. We hired a handwriting expert, who looked at a number of known signatures of the deceased party, and compared those to the signature on this purported will. Ultimately, we were successful in throwing out the will, because it was proven to be a forgery. This was the first time that the judge who heard the case had ever had a will overturned by a handwriting expert.

A second recent case in this area was interesting because of the time frame involved. A grandmother died in 1968; she gave one-half of her estate to her only son and the other half to her son as trustee for her three grandchildren. At that point, the grandchildren were all under ten years of age. Under the terms of the grandmother's will, a few hundred thousand dollars that was supposed to go to these children would be managed for their benefit during the pendency of the trust. At a certain age, the trust would be distributed to the grandchildren outright. In 2005, I met my client, who was one of the three grandchildren. He came to me because he had just learned that his father, the son of the deceased, had kept everything for himself—he had never shared any of the assets with his children, and never set up the trust that he was supposed to set up. Nor had he ever disclosed to his children that they had benefitted from grandma's estate. Basically, the father's attitude was, "I do not care what my mother says; I am going to keep everything." In the deposition, when I asked my client's father why he had not done what he was supposed to have done, he said in effect that his children did not deserve it.

Ultimately, the matter proceeded to trial. There was really no question about whether or not the father had breached his fiduciary duty as trustee, because he had basically breached every possible duty—he had essentially stolen his children's inheritance. Therefore, the question became what sort of damages are the children entitled to—i.e., can they get simple interest on the assets or reasonable growth on the assets? There is a huge difference, because if it is simple interest, you would calculate what the bank would pay you, which is now less than one percent; whereas if it is reasonable growth, then you should look at how any reasonable trustee would have invested the assets, and that is always going to be some sort of mixture of a stock and bond investment, which would result in a significantly higher long-term return.

These are the types of cases that we are encountering these days, and which are leading to a significant increase in the volume of litigation.

The Impact of the Economy and Demographics on Trust and Probate Litigation

I think that the depressed economy definitely affects this type of practice, because as the general population is hurting financially, they are going to seek out any possible way to resolve their financial issues—and litigating over family money is one of them. In addition, we have entered a period of time where we are experiencing the greatest transition of wealth from one generation to another in history—the termination of the baby boom generation, which is transferring a huge amount of money on to the next generation.

I think there is a third factor that is also leading to increased litigation in this area. It arises from the fact that there is an atmosphere of entitlement at this time. The next generation feels that they are entitled to inherit, rather than receive a gift from their relative. It almost seems like the next generation feels that it is a right to inherit and that the transferring generation has no choice in the matter.

Managing Client Expectations in Trust and Probate Litigation

Perhaps the biggest problem that I and many other practitioners in this area have is trying to manage the expectations of our clients. This is a relatively emotional practice area that is much like divorce work, where you are dealing with soon to be ex-spouses who hate each other. When you start litigating brother vs. sister, brother vs. brother, or child vs. parent, the emotions and anger levels are incredibly high. Consequently, there is a much greater chance of going all the way through litigation, because your client does not want to settle with the other side under the circumstances—and as a result, the client will often litigate their entire estate away.

For example, I had a case several years ago that involved an estate valued at slightly over $100,000. We not only had a trial about whether the will was valid, but the case went to the Court of Appeals twice, as well as the Minnesota Supreme Court. Ultimately, the entire estate was depleted by attorney's fees—and that type of result does not make sense for anybody, except for the lawyer, and even for the lawyer it is not a pleasant situation. It is always difficult when you cannot get your clients to settle. You are ultimately between a rock and a hard place—you know that it does not make sense to litigate because there is not enough money involved, but you cannot convince your client that they should not litigate. Again, in many cases the client would rather see all of the money go to the lawyers than to their brother, sister, mother, or father.

As a result, now whenever I initially meet with a client and we are talking about litigating an estate or trust matter, one of the first things that I talk about is whether it makes economic sense to fight. I explain that sometimes any settlement would be better than litigating, because if you litigate, nothing will be left. Consequently, at the outset of any case I will sit down with the client and say, "Try to be reasonable, because if you are not, nobody is going to get anything." Unfortunately, I have had only mixed success with that appeal.

Often it makes sense to appeal to the client's sense of justice. For instance, if there is a fight over an estate because one child is getting 75 percent of the estate while another child is getting only 25 percent, it may make sense for one child to give up a little bit to his sibling. Appealing to the client's sense of justice is often more effective than appealing to their economic sense—again, many clients do not care if the entire estate is eaten up in legal fees, because then the other party will not get anything either.

I have struggled with trying to find ways to manage client expectations in these cases but have not always been successful.

Mediation vs. Litigation

Over the years, I have found that the results of mediation are more mixed in this practice area than in some other areas. As previously noted, I work in a litigation firm as an estate planner where I try a number of trust and probate cases. I have found that other practice areas have a higher success rate at resolving issues through mediation. I do not think that has anything to do with the quality of the mediator; rather, it has more to do with the emotions that are involved in these cases. Again, it all goes back to that key point of managing your client's expectations. Quite often, you will be at a mediation session where the mediator and the lawyers all think that the case ought to settle, but the clients do not.

Preliminary Client Meetings and the Discovery Process

When developing a litigation strategy, I always try to resolve issues earlier rather than later. One of the most expensive portions of litigation is the discovery process, primarily because you have to figure out what your case is about before you decide whether you are going to settle or try it. Therefore, there are substantial benefits if you can try to get things resolved before you spend the majority of your client's money doing discovery—but again, you do not always know what a reasonable settlement for your client would be until you figure out what your case is really all about. Therefore, although it makes sense from an economic standpoint to settle before you get to the discovery phase, it is usually very hard to settle a case before you have done sufficient discovery.

Simply put, the discovery phase is where most good lawyering is done. Estate and trust litigation is often document intensive and the better lawyer will "discover" the key documents. Also, during discovery, you will often have to depose the lawyer who drafted the will; you have to talk to the estate owner's doctor to find out if their patient had the capacity to make a will.

I believe that being very well prepared for depositions is a key element of an effective trust and probate case strategy. If you are not well prepared for your deposition, you are probably going to miss some key information. Essentially, you need to have gone through all of the case documents before the deposition so that you know what they say. Only with a thorough understanding of the documents will you be prepared to ask the meaningful questions.

Preparation for the discovery process is also very important. After first meeting with the client, we will first try to determine what the case is about. After discussing whether an early settlement is possible, we will typically send out written discovery to the opposite side. We do our interrogatories, our request for documents, and our request for admissions. Once those come back with responses, we will schedule depositions of the people who we think are important. Additionally, if we have a witness we know is going to be good for our case, we will disclose that in our written discovery, but we will probably not schedule that person's deposition. Rather, we will list them as a potential witness, and put the onus on the other side to take depositions if they want to.

Unfortunately, because of budgetary concerns, people may not take all of the depositions that they should—which is another battle you are always fighting in this area. Over the past twenty-five years of my practice, I have been involved in very few trust and probate cases where there has been an unlimited budget to litigate. There are many cases where you know that you should do a number of things, but the budget for the case does not justify spending the money. Obviously, you should always try to do what is best for your client, but you must try to do it in as economical a manner as possible—and sometimes that is really difficult.

Recent Litigation Trends

Again, due to the bad economy, more people are filing trust and probate claims. Therefore, we are facing a larger volume of litigation, but with the budgetary cuts that we are currently experiencing and are going to have in the future, there is less capacity in the courts to try these cases than ever before. Here in Hennepin County, we have a probate court judge and probate court referees who handle probate and trust litigation. However, both of the referees are of an age where they are going to be retiring soon, and instead of hiring two replacements, they are hiring two half-time replacements. Therefore, we are going to have the equivalent of a judge and a referee going forward, instead of a judge and two referees. Consequently, there is going to be significantly less capacity for the court to hear probate and trust litigation matters.

Minnesota is not alone in having budget issues. Other jurisdictions will have the same problems. Therefore, there will be cases that you may want to try, but it is going to take longer to get them to trial, simply because there are not enough judicial officers.

Best Practices for Handling Complex Elements of a Trust and Probate Case

One of the most complicated elements of a trust and probate case is the volume of documents you have to analyze, and sometimes some issues are more complicated than others are. As noted, you may need to talk to the lawyer who drafted the will, or you may need to talk to the deceased person's doctor, as they will be able to give you a pretty clear idea of whether the person had sufficient capacity. The trust case that I handled involving the grandmother's bequest for her grandchildren was complex not only because there were many different types of assets that we had to try to trace, but also because of the time frame involved. For instance, we had to look through bank ledgers that were forty years old.

In some cases, the issues behind a case make it especially complex. In Minnesota, you can go through a process that allows you to get a will changed if a conservator agrees with your argument, and the court approves the change. We recently handled a case in which our client originally claimed that the will was invalid, either because of lack of capacity on the part of the deceased, or because he was unduly influenced. However, when we did our discovery and I talked to the lawyer who drafted the will, it became apparent to me that we really did not have a very strong claim. Consequently, as the case progressed, we changed our theory to make it clear that the will that was currently in place was not the will that the deceased had wanted, but rather, there was undue influence in preventing him from changing the will—a cause of action that does not currently exist. Therefore, we were basically asking the court to recognize a novel cause of action. Ultimately, the District Court was unwilling to recognize our cause of action. The Court of Appeals agreed, saying that only the legislature or the Supreme Court could do so. Therefore, we did not succeed in our claim.

New Technologies for Managing Documents

Fortunately, with respect to cases that are complex because of a significant volume of documents, there are new document control systems that work really well. Such systems allow you to easily scan documents and conduct word searches, and in doing so, you can minimize the volume of the documents that you need to utilize. Our firm has a good technical staff, and it is a tremendous benefit to have people who can assist you in the area of document control and management.

When I started practicing law, we did not even have desktop computers. Our secretaries used typewriters and made carbon copies of documents. Simply stated, the practice of law has changed tremendously in the last twenty-five years. In the past, you would have to read an entire stack of documents, and you would then put Post-it notes on the key documents, make copies of those documents, and use them as exhibits at trial. Now, however, with advanced document control systems, the necessary documents are easily scanned into a database and the documents are easily and quickly reviewed using keywords, and you can then pull out the appropriate documents simply by pushing a button on the computer. I have found that this process can significantly cut the timeline for cases where there are many documents involved. At my firm, we've invested in the technology that helps us to deliver the value that clients now demand.

Looking to the Future

Looking ahead, I think there is going to be more stress from the courts on attempting alternative dispute resolution (ADR) in trust and probate cases. The courts are going to have fewer people who are able and willing to handle litigation matters. By necessity there will need to be different ways of resolving issues. At the same time, I think that there is going to be more litigation rather than less litigation, which is going to compound that problem. That is all related to the demographics of the increasing number of estates transitioning from one generation to another, and the fact that the economy is pushing people to litigate more. As a result, there is going to be a crunch in terms of the number of people that are going to have the courts available to them.

Clearly, the huge number of dollars that are transferring from this generation to the next is a motivating factor in today's trust and probate cases. Another big motivating factor is petty jealousies between siblings that often go back fifty years. While the parents are living the children seem to get along okay, but issues emerge after a parent's death. Also, when one spouse dies the other parent often becomes more susceptible to influence. For example, if the parent is seventy years old, their spouse is deceased, and they are starting to struggle with some cognitive loss, the survivor often becomes dependent upon one of the children. That can result in the parent favoring the "helpful" child more than the others or in the child attempting to help himself to the parent's estate simply because they have access. This has been called the "vulnerable adult" issue—i.e., an elderly person who is susceptible to influence, and a family member or a non-family member is taking advantage of that person. It is a crime to financially abuse a vulnerable adult, but the authorities are often not willing to investigate or prosecute these cases, which is unfortunate. Consequently, a number of end-of-life issues are going to become bigger problems in the coming years.

Final Thoughts

One of my biggest struggles in my practice, as previously noted, is trying to make clients look at things reasonably from the start. It is important to point out that litigating against family members is not a pleasant thing. Life is too short, in my opinion, for siblings to fight over money; yet animosity can be so great that people are often unwilling to resolve issues. I can often see from the start where things are going to be heading in these cases, and although I will explain to my clients that they are going to spend almost as much litigating a case as they are going to benefit from it if they succeed, they still may not accept my counsel.

There is one significant benefit to this litigation field. There is generally a difference between lawyers who litigate in the probate and trust area and the general litigation world. It is a less aggressive, more genteel practice for the most part, which makes it more pleasant for the lawyers. Attorneys are not bringing unnecessary discovery motions simply to harass; attorneys are not being unreasonable at depositions; people let you ask questions and give you the answers you want without arguing about every issue. My litigation practice is thus more pleasing than those of many of my partners. It is my hope that the trend continues.

Key Takeaways

- One of the most difficult aspects of being a lawyer in this practice area is trying to manage client expectations. As a result, whenever you first meet with a client about litigating an estate or trust matter, you should discuss whether it makes economic sense to litigate. Sometimes any settlement would be better than litigating, because if you litigate, there may be no estate left.
- There are substantial benefits if you can try to get things resolved before you spend the majority of your client's money doing discovery—but again, you do not always know what a reasonable settlement for your client would be until you figure out what your case is really all about.
- There are many cases where you know that you should undertake a number of discovery functions, but the budget for the case does not justify spending the money. Obviously, you should always try

to do what is best for your client, but you must try to do it in as economical a manner as possible—and sometimes that is really difficult.

- With advanced document control systems, you can have all the necessary documents scanned into your computer system; you can then have a paralegal review all of the documents using keywords that you give to them; and you can then pull out the appropriate documents simply by pushing a button on the computer. This process can significantly cut the timeline for cases where there are many documents involved.

For more than twenty years, Timothy W. Ridley, a partner at Meagher & Geer PLLP, has focused his practice on the preparation of wills, trusts and estate plans for individuals—as well as related litigation.

Mr. Ridley has been named a Super Lawyer® and is listed as a Top 40 Estate Planning and Probate Law Attorney by Minnesota Law & Politics *magazine. After consulting with clients to determine their personal and financial goals and objectives, Mr. Ridley helps them structure the estate plan that best meets their needs. To accomplish this, he looks for the most efficient methods for transferring the client's assets—with a goal of tax minimization and simplicity.*

Mr. Ridley offers a special depth of experience in cases involving breach of fiduciary duty in the management of probate, estates, and trusts. On the plaintiff side, he represents estate and trust beneficiaries. On the defendant side, he represents personal representatives, trustees, and guardians. He also serves as expert witness both for and against fiduciaries. Mr. Ridley also represents small and mid-sized business owners in their business transactions and disputes. Outside the office, Mr. Ridley is a board member of several charitable organizations.

Mr. Ridley is a member of the Minnesota State Bar Association, the Probate and Trust Law Section, and the Hennepin County Bar Association.

Proactive Measures and Key Concerns for the Trust and Probate Attorney

Ray J. Koenig III

Member

Clark Hill PLC

ASPATORE

The Reasons for the Rise in Trust and Probate Litigation: Demographics and Increasing Complexity

For a variety of reasons, it seems that the "baby boomer" generation is the most litigious generation the world has known. The baby boomers' parents—the so-called "greatest generation"—are also the wealthiest generation to date; they have more money than anybody ever had in the past. Now those parents are becoming disabled or dying and their children—the baby boomers—are fighting over their estates. Consequently, we have a situation where the most litigious generation is fighting over the funds from the wealthiest generation. This combination has led to a dramatic growth in probate and trust litigation over the years—a trend which is only going to continue. The first set of boomers just turned sixty-five and the boomers' parents are well into their eighties. The boomers' parents will begin dying in large numbers, which will only add to more litigation.

Another cause for greater litigation is that estate planning techniques have become a lot more sophisticated over the years—but sometimes people do not know what they are doing when they are setting up or administering these complex structures. In fact, unless you are a bank or a large institution, it can be difficult to serve as trustee or executor of one of these new trusts that contain sophisticated terms and vehicles. Due to lack of knowledge, people are making mistakes, which lead to more errors and more breach of fiduciary duty actions. Essentially, the more complicated things are, the more litigation there is.

Causes of Actions in Estate and Trust Contests

There are three primary causes of action in will and trust contests: lack of mental capacity, undue influence, and tortious interference with an expectancy. The facts of the case will determine whether one or all three causes of action ought to be plead. Below is a brief outline of the elements necessary to plead each cause of action.

Lack of Mental Capacity

The threshold for sufficient mental capacity to execute a will or testamentary trust is quite low. The contestant must establish that the testator/settlor lacked the mental capacity to (1) know the nature and extent of his property; (2) know the natural objects of his bounty; and (3) have the ability to make a disposition of his property in accordance with some plan formed in his mind. In order to contest the execution of an *inter vivos* trust based on lack of mental capacity, the contestant must establish that the settlor lacked the capacity contract. In other words, you need to have a higher level of capacity to execute an *inter vivos* trust than a will or testamentary trust.

Undue Influence

Undue influence is present where the testator or settlor is prevented from disposing of his property in a manner he or she chooses. Instead, his or her free will is so overcome that the disposition of his or her property reflects the wishes of the wrongdoer rather than the testator/settlor. Undue influence is rebuttably presumed if the contestant can establish the following: (1) a fiduciary relationship existed between the testator/settlor and the person who benefits under the will/trust; (2) the primary beneficiaries were in a position to dominate and control the dependent testator/settlor; (3) the testator/settlor reposed trust and confidence in these beneficiaries; and (4) the beneficiaries were instrumental in the procurement or preparation of the will or trust. This presumption is rebuttable, however.

Tortious Interference with an Expectancy

To state a cause of action for tortious interference with an expectancy the plaintiff must allege: (1) the existence of an expectancy; (2) the defendant's intentional interference with this expectancy; (3) the interference involving conduct tortious in itself, such as fraud, duress, or undue influence; (4) reasonable certainly that the devise to the plaintiff would have been received but for the defendant's interference; and (5) damages. In Illinois, if the contestant could receive adequate relief through a will contest and he was aware of his claim prior to the expiration of the limitations period, he must seek redress through a will contest. *Inter vivos* transfers, however, cannot be recovered through a will contest. Thus, if the contestant believes someone tortiously interfered with his expectancy to receive certain assets, such as insurance policies or a 401k, he may file a tortious interference action against that alleged tortfeasor.

Breaches of Fiduciary Duty by Executors and Trustees

A fiduciary is "a person who has a legal duty, created by his undertaking, to act for the benefit of another in matters connected with his undertaking." Stephen H. Gifis, *Black's Law Dictionary* (5th ed., 2003). A fiduciary relationship may exist as a matter of law or as a matter of fact. Examples of fiduciary relationships that exist as a matter of law are: a trustee of a trust, an executor of a will, and an agent under power of attorney. Courts have found a fiduciary relationship to exist in fact where, for example, an individual took care of an elderly person's health care and finances even though power of attorney documents were never executed. A fiduciary's duties include *inter alia*: using reasonable care, skill, and caution, serving loyally and impartially, and not delegating his or her responsibilities.

In regard to trusts, a trustee has fiduciary obligations to the trust beneficiaries. A trustee may be sued for breach of fiduciary duty for, *inter alia*, failing to invest trust assets prudently, not looking out for the best interests of all the beneficiaries, taking money from the trust, or failing to account to trust beneficiaries.

In regard to wills, an executor has fiduciary obligations to the beneficiaries of the estate. The fiduciary may be sued for breach of fiduciary duty for, *inter alia*, failing to collect all estate assets, self-dealing (i.e., selling the estate-owned home to himself for below fair market value); or failing to administer the estate according to the terms of the will.

The Impact of the Current Economic Landscape on Trust and Estate Litigation

The economy has not had a negative impact on my practice. My business has actually increased, but that could have more to do with the trajectory of my career than with the actual economy. I am a relatively young partner, and my business is expected to grow. However, I have noticed that there have been fewer cases involving huge sums of money in the past year, largely because many of the big estates are not as big as they used to be due to the real estate crash and market instability. Likewise, there tends to be less willingness to litigate what I would consider to be mid-sized estates because of the cost-benefit analysis. Many of the cases that would have been brought a few years ago are not being brought now, simply because the litigants do not have the money to fund litigation and because the potential payoff is not as great.

One area of estate litigation that has increased dramatically is the number of breach of fiduciary duty cases brought against banks who serve as trustees. Trust beneficiaries want someone to blame for the downturn in the economy and the reduction in their interest income or the total value of their trust. Since they cannot sue the chairman of the Federal Reserve or Congress, they are suing the bank that served as trustee of the family's trust. I defend banks in these types of cases. These cases are particularly sticky because the issue is whether the bank acted in accordance with the prudent investor standard when investing trust assets during the recent real estate and stock market crash. Under these circumstances, it is difficult to determine whether a corporate fiduciary was acting imprudently. Was it really imprudent for the corporate trustee to invest trust assets in the stock market? Can the corporate trustee be liable to the beneficiaries for failing to cash out before the crash?

Jurisdictional Considerations

Probate and trust litigation are practically always done at the state level. All of my cases, for example, are in Illinois. For this reason, you must learn the laws and customs that govern the state and county you are practicing in. For example, in Illinois, we have what is called a substitution of judges by right, which some states do not. Essentially, each party is allowed to suggest a judge's substitution. Therefore, if you are not familiar with the judge in your case you have to research their previous rulings and talk to other people about the judge, and then discuss with your client if you want certain matters brought in that courtroom.

While there are state statutes that govern where I can file suit (i.e., a will contest must be brought in the county where the decedent died), when I have the choice I prefer trying cases in Cook County. Of course, that is not to say that the judges in other counties are bad. In fact, the trust is far from it. However, they do not see the volume and breadth of cases the judges in Cook County see. In the smaller counties, where judges handle more than just probate, attorneys generally have to educate the judge more so than we do in Cook County because we have judges that deal exclusively with probate.

While estate and trust litigation is typically handled on the state level, it is important to stay abreast of trends in other states. I have partners across the country, and we discuss issues we are seeing and how courts are resolving them. Communicating with attorneys outside Illinois allows me to learn new strategies and arguments that may be appropriate for my cases here in Illinois.

Components of Trust and Probate Litigation Strategy

Client's Goals and Key Motivations

The first motivation in most trust and probate litigation is money, and the second is probably a person's ego or desire to be vindicated on "principle." I have found that whenever someone says that he or she is engaging in litigation to defend a principle, it is usually because of his or her ego. The third motivation is some combination of affection, emotion, and family history. For example, clients often tell me that there is no way their mother could have wanted one of their siblings to receive more of an inheritance because she always told the client that he or she was her favorite. The person usually initiates litigation to defend the belief that he or she was the favorite and some wrongdoing had to have occurred for his or her mother to leave so much to the other siblings rather than to him or her.

At the outset of any trust and probate litigation, I always try to identify the goals of my client—i.e., what is it they want, and what is it that they expect to achieve. From that point, I figure out what is legally possible. I do this because what the client wants and what you can actually legally achieve are often very different things. As stated earlier, many of these cases are driven by emotions: some clients just want to know that their mother loved all of her children equally, but their mother is dead. Other times the client really wants their sibling to apologize, and that is just not going to happen, whether we settle or win at trial.

I always advise my clients to think seriously about whether or not they want to bring litigation; it is emotionally and financially draining. If the client will end up spending $200,000 on litigation, and the most they can get out of it is $300,000, they need to decide if they should go through with it. Some will choose to proceed because they are emotionally invested in vindicating what they believe to be the decedent's true intent. Others will be more pragmatic and may recognize it is not worth the fight.

Therefore, when I build a litigation strategy, it is important to identify the client's goals and what is legally possible. Then I talk to the client about those issues, and try to get them back down to earth if necessary.

Educating the Client and Setting Expectations

Client education is extremely important in these cases. If a client's expectations are improperly managed, you will have a very unhappy client. In fact, I will decline cases where the client has unreasonable expectations about what he or she can or cannot do in a will or trust contest.

When working with a client on a probate or trust matter, it is important to listen and never condescend. The counseling process is part therapy and part education. If you seriously consider the client's feelings or emotions, you will often be able to recognize what is really motivating them in bringing or defending the litigation. You have to spend some non-billable time on the phone with the client discussing their motivation. They have generally been thinking about these issues for a long time, and they want to share their feelings with someone who cares—their attorney.

I tend to not have to educate bank clients as much because these clients are professionals who do this for a living. They frequently know almost as much about the law as I do. Again, however, individual clients typically have no background in estates and trusts and require continuous education on the law and the process of estate/trust litigation.

I try to make a client wait a couple of days before deciding to move forward with non-mandatory litigation. It is crucial for the long term. It is not necessarily the best business decision to rope a client into doing something they do not necessarily want to do, because, in the end, they are not going to want to pay for it. Litigation is a huge emotional and financial investment; the client has to be committed. Therefore, I try to make them wait a couple days before they make the decision to go forward and that very rarely backfires. In fact, it usually allows the client to come up with more questions, and only then will they be ready to decide whether they are going to actually commit to the litigation.

Stay Organized and Simplify Your Case

In order to succeed in these cases, you need to know your facts and the law very well. Keep yourself and your facts organized. The discovery process will lead to an overload of information, so it is important to be organized from day one. Create timelines and summaries and always have a running list of questions that you will go back to check and recheck. This will help you narrow down your case and stay focused on what you need to prove. In every case, you must prove to a judge or a jury that your facts demonstrate that only one legal outcome is appropriate. In order to do this, you must pinpoint your goal and simplify your case. Judges and juries respond to simplicity.

You want to give the judge and jury an explanation they can easily agree with. If you take a complex issue and make it easy for them to understand, it is easier for them to agree with you. This strategy is sometimes easier to achieve with a jury than with a judge. The judge may have used such strategies themselves and may reject them. Regardless, it is always a good idea to simplify your case as much as possible.

Achieve Early Victories

It is important to consider what you can do to bring about an early settlement that is favorable to your client—and one way to do that is to try to quickly obtain early moral and legal victories. I will often try to somewhat demoralize the other side by defeating any unfounded claims as early as possible and poking holes in their facts. Basically, I try to get rid of the big dramatic elements in the other party's case while attempting to score an early legal victory. Even a small victory develops momentum, which will make the other side reconsider the strength of their case. Each party comes into litigation thinking that they know the truth and they are going to win. The mentality is: *how could a judge or jury ever decide otherwise?* However, you have to show the other side as well as the judge or jury that the case could indeed be decided otherwise. You must attempt to achieve as many of those victories as early as possible. All of these early efforts will allow you (and the judge) to properly assess the strengths of the case. By achieving early victories in court and persuading the other side of the strength of your case, you are educating the judge and making them familiar with your side of the story—this helps in the long run.

I will always try to bring an action in a way that leverages the strengths of my client's case. My goal in every case is not necessarily to win at trial. I want to win, but I do not defend litigation based solely on how it would play out at trial. Early victories typically allow me to reach a settlement with the other side, making trial unnecessary.

Educate the Judge

It is important to educate the judge on the simple theory behind your case early as possible. For example, in some instances it may be important to file a certain motion, not because you absolutely believe you will win the motion, but because it is an opportunity to educate the judge on the facts or theory of the case. I have also filed certain motions in order to educate the judge on the unsavory tactics of my opposing counsel, so that the judge is on notice of whom she or he is dealing with. Educating the judge on the facts benefits my client in the long run.

Preparing for Litigation: Building your Team:

Legal Assistants

Some of the best litigators have amazing assistants. In fact, in my opinion, you cannot become a successful attorney, especially in litigation, without an assistant who understands the basics of the law, gets along well with clients and opposing counsel, and can handle many of the procedural aspects of these cases, thus alleviating the responsibility and worry from you.

Associates/Partners

Associates and paralegals are crucial in a successful trust and estate litigation practice. The number of such people on a case varies with the complexity of the case. I will handle a smaller case myself, but there are some cases where I have four partners and three or four associates working with me, because the case is complex and involves a lot of work.

I benefit from working in a larger firm where I can have other partners look at the issues in my case to get an outlook from a fresh set of eyes. Because probate and trust litigation may touch on many areas of the law, I will also bring in a partner who specializes in tax or real estate or whatever the case requires in order to provide my client the best possible team to litigate his or her case.

Advice and Counsel from Attorneys outside the Case

When you are working on a case with people in your firm, you sometimes tend to suffer from group think. For example, associates may adopt my interpretation as their own, rather than thinking about an issue for themselves. In an effort to avoid group think, I have been known to retain outside attorneys to analyze a specific subject or specific issues. Of course, it will cost the client a little more, but not too much more, because they would have paid me for that time anyway. Most importantly, I will be able to get a different perspective from someone who is not immersed in the case, which can bring a favorable outcome to the client.

In addition, the probate attorneys in Chicago are a pretty collegial bunch who are often willing to give a few minutes of their time to analyze an issue or recommend an expert referral.

Experts

Outside experts are extremely important in trust and estate litigation. Since the testator/settlor's mental capacity is often at issue, it is generally necessary to present his or her physician or another medical expert who can discuss his or her mental capacity and medical condition. Physicians and nurses are frequently retained for this reason.

In addition, forensic accountants are frequently used as experts. For example, if a trust owns shares of a family business, an accountant may be brought in to analyze the value of the business. Similarly, if a trustee sued for breach of fiduciary duty, compiling a complete trust accounting and analyzing the trustee's actions with respect to the trust's assets will also require an expert accountant.

I frequently rely on word of mouth for finding the appropriate expert for a case. Over time, I have developed good relationships with some doctors and accountants, who I will call on since I know and respect their level of professionalism. I tend to avoid hiring experts who have referred me business because I do not want any bias to affect my client's case.

Complex Trust and Probate Cases

Successive Documents

What I consider a complex trust or probate case is a case that involves a lot of successive documents—i.e., the client executed a new trust every year for fifteen years, and they were either unduly influenced or lacked capacity to execute those documents over the last six years. Therefore, you have to contest six successive documents. That usually entails six successive trials to contest the validity of each document. That gets very expensive, which usually encourages settlement.

Tax Issues

If a case involves trust construction, undue influence, or lack of capacity matter, *and* taxes are at issue, the case frequently becomes infinitely more complex. Our tax code has changed a great deal over the years, and when estate documents have been executed in different years, the challenge involves trying to figure out why the client did what they did, and how the tax law has changed since that time. Basically, you are trying to argue to the judge that the client did certain things for a particular reason, and that makes the case a bit more complex—i.e., if when the client executed their estate documents, they were trying to take advantage of a law under the tax scheme that existed at that time, which may be very different than the present laws.

Multiple Parties and Conflicts of Interest

Multiple invested parties with conflicting interests also make for a complex trust or probate case. I have had cases where there were fifteen attorneys, all representing different clients and with different agendas. In such a case, I may be aligned with half the parties and against half the parties on certain motions. Resolving such a case takes incredible organizational skills and a good team.

The Fine Line in Breach of Fiduciary Duty Cases

Another type of complex case is if a beneficiary files a breach of fiduciary action and the facts are unclear as to whether there was in fact a breach of duty. Many of these cases involve investment decisions that were made over the last four or five years. Issues in these types of cases are whether a particular bank should or should not have taken a certain action, and whether its action or inaction constitutes a breach of fiduciary duty. These cases are becoming more complex, because in the past when the market was always going up and you lost money, it was easier to prove a breach, but in this economy, a loss of 10 to 15 percent may or may not necessarily be a breach. Therefore, you are dealing with a lot more financial and economic data than in most cases, which often requires the use of an expert to sift through it and draw conclusions.

Recent Trends and Changes in the Law

A Tortious Interference with an Expectancy Action May Be Filed After the Six Month Period for Filing a Will Contest Has Past

The Illinois Supreme Court held in *In Re Estate of Ellis* that a tortious interference with expectancy action, in certain circumstances, may be filed after the six month statute of limitations to file a will contest has expired. *In re Estate of Ellis,* 236 Ill. 2d. 45, 923 N.E.2d 237 (2009). In *Ellis,* the decedent named Shriners Hospitals for Children as beneficiary under her 1964 will, provided she had no descendants. In 1999, the decedent wrote a new will naming her pastor as the sole beneficiary of the estate. The decedent died in 2003 with no descendants and her 1999 will was admitted to probate. Shriners did not learn of their interest under the 1964 will until 2006, well after Illinois' six month claim period to file a will contest had run. Shriners brought suit against the estate alleging, among other things, tortious interference with an expectancy.

Shriners alleged that the reverend knowingly interfered with Shriners' expectancy under the 1964 will by abusing his position of trust by unduly influencing the decedent to execute a new will. Shriners alleged that but for the reverend's interference, Shriners would have received the estate. The lower courts dismissed the claim as untimely because it was not filed within the six month limitation period for filing a will contest that they applied to tortious claims. The lower court reasoned that the legislature could not have intended to bar a will contest after six months but permit identical allegations to proceed in through a tort action. This had been the general understanding for years.

The Supreme Court reversed, finding that a tortious interference claim is not limited by the six month limitation period in the Probate Act because the six month limitation period explicitly states that it only applies to will contests. Moreover, the purpose of a will contest, even if the allegations are the same as a tortious interference action, is entirely different. A successful will contest will set aside a decedent's will, whereas a tortious interference action is directed toward the individual tortfeasor and if successful will result in a judgment against the individual defendant. The Illinois Supreme Court noted that had Shriners known about their interest early enough to file within the six month limitation period they would not have waited until after the period ran to file their tort action.

In sum, the Illinois Supreme Court held that while a tortious interference action is not governed by the six month limitation period, if the contestant knew about the tort and could have brought the action during the six month limitation period and received adequate relief through a will contest, the contestant is required to file a will contest instead of a tortious interference action. If, however, a will contest will not provide adequate relief, then the contestant can proceed with his or her tort action. The Illinois Supreme Court allowed Shriners' claim to proceed because Shriners did not learn about their expectancy until well after the limitation period, and a will contest would not have provided it adequate relief because numerous assets were transferred to the reverend outside of probate.

This case is important because it expands the opportunity to litigate estates. Prior to *Ellis*, most practitioners and trial court judges understood the law to be that any action to contest a will or trust, or to bring a tortious interference action, had to be filed within the six month limitation period. While the Illinois Supreme Court attempted to narrow their decision to the facts of *Ellis*, the case has nevertheless opened the door for parties to litigate estates well after they have been administered based on a claim of tortious interference, provided the contestant did not have notice within the six month limitation period. As a result, attorneys who administer estates may want to consider giving notice to any individual or entity known to have had an interest in a prior will in order to foreclose on an individual or entity bringing an action well past the six month limitation period. Of course, providing them that notice may invite litigation as well.

This case obviously benefits litigators in that it expands our opportunity to bring a cause of action. However, litigators nevertheless need to mindful when bringing such a case. Litigators need to consider whether his or her client will be able to gather sufficient evidence to plead and prove tortious conduct like fraud or undue influence. The longer it has been from the date of the purported fraudulent transaction, the more difficult it is to prove. Additionally, it is important to consider the likelihood of recovering the assets allegedly subject to interference. Is your client actually going to be able to recover or is your client going to get a judgment against an insolvent tortfeasor? This will affect whether your client wants to proceed with the case.

Pre-Death Will and Trust Amendments and Contests

I am increasingly seeing fights over who should be appointed guardian of a disabled person in order to propose estate planning documents, or more commonly, to amend the existing estate plan of the disabled person. In other words, why wait until the person dies when you can fight over their estate while they are still alive? Recently, the First District of Illinois chimed in on this issue. In *In Re Estate of Henry*, the First District held that individuals cannot contest a will or the validity of a revocable *inter vivos* trust agreement in which a legacy is provided by the settlor's will until after the testator/settler is deceased. *In re Estate of Henry,* 396 Ill. App. 3d 88; 919 N.E.2d 33 (1st Dist. 2009). In this case, Richard Henry was adjudicated disabled in 2006 and a guardian of his estate and person were appointed. The guardian of the estate subsequently filed a citation action against the disabled person's caretaker that resulted in a finding that the disabled person lacked decisional capacity since December 31, 2003 and his caretaker had misappropriated more than $1 million from the disabled person. After this ruling, the guardian of the estate petitioned the court to execute a new codicil, will, and trust on behalf of the disabled person claiming his 2004 will was not a valid expression of his intent because its primary beneficiary was the caretaker and a nephew. The disabled person's prior 1999 will left most of his estate to charity. The guardian of the estate basically wanted to reinstate the terms of the 1999 will. The court permitted the guardian of the estate to execute the estate planning documents, thereby removing the caretaker and nephew's interest therein. The caretaker and nephew appealed.

The First District dismissed the caretaker and nephew's appeal holding that they did not have standing. The court held they did not have standing to challenge the trial court's order on behalf of the disabled person because they were not the disabled person's guardian. Additionally, the court held that they did not have standing to challenge the order on their own behalf because they did not have an injury: a will is not legally operative until after death. Since the nephew and the caretaker did not have a property interest until after the testator dies, they, like all the other legatees, had to wait until after the testator's death to challenge the disposition of his property. Similarly, the court held that beneficiaries of a revocable *inter vivos* trust, which is a legatee under a will, lack standing to challenge amendments made by the settlor during his lifetime. The court cited section 8-1(f) of the Probate Act which specifically states that "an action to set aside or contest the validity of a revocable *inter vivos* trust agreement or declaration of trust to which a legacy is provided by the settlor's will which is admitted to probate shall be commenced within and not after the time to contest the validity of a will."

This case is important because it reaffirms that a party does not have standing to file a will contest or contest the validity of a revocable *inter vivos* trust agreement in which a legacy is provided by the settlor's will until after the testator/settler is deceased. Recently there has been a trend in people attempting to modify an individual's estate plan after he or she has lost capacity but before the person has died. Some people simply come to court and try to contest the will and/or revocable *inter vivos* trust as invalid during the settlor/testator's lifetime. This is clearly not permissible under the Probate Act, which the holding in *Henry* reinforces.

The proper procedure for modifying the estate plan of an individual who does not have the mental capacity to modify it himself or herself is to petition for guardianship over the individual. Once a guardian of the estate is in place, the guardian may petition the court to modify the disabled person's estate plan. I have petitioned the probate court to modify estate plans on numerous occasions. In one case, the disabled person left all of his non-probate assets to the sister with whom he was particularly close. He did not have a will, and as a result, his probate estate would pass by intestacy. Based on his selection of sister as beneficiary of all of his non-probate assets and the fact that he did not have a relationship with his other siblings, I successfully petitioned the court to name his sister as his sole beneficiary of his estate. Cases are not always as simple or obvious as the example I just provided or the facts in Henry. If a client comes to you with a goal of becoming guardian simply to try to modify new estate planning documents for the alleged disabled person, carefully consider whether his plan is appropriate for the alleged disabled person based on the facts of the case.

Divorce Decrees

Another trend that I see in probate these days—and was mentioned to me by a sitting probate judge—is enforcement of divorce decrees in decedents' estates. If a spouse is not meeting their obligations under their divorce decree, the surviving ex-spouse or children who are entitled to certain benefits are bringing claims in the decedents' estates. Therefore, some probate judges have had to learn family law quickly.

Settlement Structures

Settlement structures for trust and probate litigation in today's economy often depend on the type of case and the individuals involved. These cases frequently involve the sale of real estate. Recently I have noticed a lot fewer structured payouts. On the other hand, a few years back during the real estate boom, people were more comfortable with structured settlements or getting third parties involved to finance settlements.

Emerging Practices to Prevent Probate Litigation

What Estate Planners Can Do

The estate planner is the first line of defense in trust and probate litigation. The estate planner should always meet with the client alone when working on their estate plan to make sure that this is what the client really wants. The estate planner should take steps to ensure that the execution of the will or trust cannot be questioned. For example, if the testator is going to leave everything to his niece, the niece should not be contacting the estate planner to arrange the execution of the will, nor should the niece be driving the testator to the estate planner's office. These raise red flags that perhaps the testator was unduly influenced by his niece. During the meetings with the client, it is important that the estate planner take detailed notes, because they will end up being a useful tool if the estate planning documents are litigated and the estate planner is required to testify regarding the documents he or she drafted.

Estate planners need to take particular caution when they are advising an older client with memory impairments. Just because a client is old and forgetful does not mean he or she is incapable of executing estate planning documents. In regard to mental incompetency, a red flag exists where a client knows you are her lawyer, but cannot remember your name, or the client knows where she lives, but she would not be able to find her way home on her own, or she thinks her house is worth $200,000 when it is worth $1.2 million. All of those symptoms are potential red flags for future probate litigation. Therefore, the attorney of such a client should commemorate the fact that she has capacity by having her see a doctor who can confirm in writing that the client was competent at the time she executed her estate plan.

Doctrine of Election

I have found that many people are taking offensive action to prevent trust and probate litigation these days. In Illinois, for example, we have what is called the doctrine of election, which is like a waiver. If someone dies, and you are a beneficiary of his or her will or trust, and you then receive at least part of your designated benefit from that document, you are later prohibited from challenging the trust or will. Consequently, as soon as someone dies and the executor or trustee assumes fiduciary status, he or she should try to make partial distributions from the estate or trust as soon as possible.

For instance, if someone is supposed to ultimately inherit $250,000 plus a seashell collection, the trustee should give that beneficiary the seashell collection right away, or perhaps $5,000. The trustee has no obligation to tell them why they are doing that. Essentially, making a partial distribution from a trust or will early on makes it much harder for a beneficiary to contest the trust or will at a later time. This emerging tactic has been used by some of the smarter people in this area for quite a while, and many other practitioners are now catching on.

The Role of Technology and the Discovery Process

Today, every piece of information that comes into our office is basically made part of our technological database, and we have various ways of storing it, manipulating it, organizing it, and linking it so that we can do internal searches of all of the discovery documents within minutes—a process that would have taken hours or days in the past. Also, in terms of organization, there is now less fear of losing a case in a situation where you realize that you forgot about or cannot find a document at the last minute. It is interesting how the more paperless we become, the more documents are produced in discovery. Thus, while there is more to sift through and organize, there are luckily better tools to do both.

Final Thoughts

Stay Current and Build Relationships

Most probate cases are settled; therefore, you do not hear about what transpires in those cases, other than by talking to your colleagues or by attending continuing legal education programs. Consequently, many of the strategies I have learned in my practice stem from conversations with my colleagues, including some former opposing counsel. I cannot stress enough the importance of having strong relationships with people in your field. I have learned much of what I know from people whom I argue cases with and against. When we are not opposing each other, we are swapping ideas and information. Learning from other attorneys in your field benefits both your practice and theirs. In fact, I have found that the more successful and knowledgeable attorneys tend to be the ones that most people like. Sometimes you have to play the bully to pursue your client's goals, but that does not mean you have to do it all the time.

This practice area requires that you have an understanding about many different areas of the law, including civil litigation, estate planning, probate, mental health law, and tax law. It is important that you attend continuing education seminars and solicit help from attorneys and other experts who have an expertise in an area that is important to your case so you can competently represent your client. For example, in a lack of mental capacity case you will have to understand medicine because a physician is inevitably going to be a witness. If you are going to be an excellent estate litigator, you should know more than your witness does, which frequently means learning the medical issues in your case with the same degree of competency that an excellent personal injury attorney would.

Continuing education is important because the law is constantly changing. It is frustrating to go up against an attorney who does not know what she or he is doing. Unfortunately, we see that a lot, especially as this area grows. Conversely, it is always good to go up against a great attorney, because you get a better outcome for all parties. When you are negotiating with someone who knows what could happen in court, they can advise their client correctly; whereas if you go up against someone who may only know a little about these issues, they may be giving their client awful advice that is causing them not to settle on a certain issue. In such a situation, my client may wind up winning at trial, but it will also cost them another $50,000, whereas if we were dealing with an attorney who knows what they are doing, the case would not go that far.

Maintain Client Satisfaction

Finally, it is crucial that your client feels a part of the team and is on board for what lies ahead. Litigation is extremely unpredictable—your client needs to be aware that there is no guarantee. I find that the best way to keep a client happy with my service is to maintain constant communication. I always try to take a client's call, and if I cannot, then I call them back as soon as possible. Each and every client should feel like their case is your number one priority. Litigators must be good at balancing a multitude of cases that all have unexpected twists and turns. Because of the unpredictable nature of litigation, it is important that litigators do their best to control what they can: client expectations and client relationships are in the attorney's hands at all times.

Key Takeaways

- At the outset of any trust and probate litigation, I always try to identify the goals of my client. When working with a client on a probate or trust matter, it is important to listen and never condescend.
- It is important to consider what you can do to bring about an early settlement that is favorable to your client—and one way to do that is try to quickly obtain early moral and legal victories. I will often try to somewhat demoralize the other side by poking big holes in their claims, and try to defeat the most ridiculous issues they are bringing up.
- A successful attorney, especially in litigation, needs an assistant who understands the basics of the law, who gets along well with clients and opposing counsel, and who is able to handle all the procedural aspects of these cases so that you do not have to worry about them. Hiring outside experts, such as medical professionals, is also important.

The two main causes of action in trust and probate litigation are lack of capacity and undue influence. A good estate planner will look at the elements of those causes of action and have a doctor verify the client's mental state, if necessary.

Ray J. Koenig III is a member in Clark Hill PC's Litigation Practice Group in its Chicago office. He practices in the areas of probate litigation, trust litigation, fiduciary litigation, elder law, estate planning, and estate administration, with an emphasis on will, trust, guardianship, and advance directive contests and other fiduciary litigation. Mr. Koenig has represented individuals, families, financial institutions, medical institutions, and governmental organizations in all areas of his practice.

Mr. Koenig has extensive trial, appellate, and mediation experience in state and federal courts. He is frequently appointed guardian ad litem and defense counsel by judges in guardianship cases, and has been appointed special administrator in probate matters. Mr. Koenig has also been appointed Illinois Special Assistant Attorney General in numerous matters.

Mr. Koenig is very involved in the communities to which he belongs. He is frequently published in professional, scholarly, and community publications. He is also a frequent speaker at seminars and events for the community, his peers, and other professionals. Mr. Koenig is also proud to serve on the boards of multiple charitable organizations.

Mr. Koenig earned his bachelor's degree from Michigan State University. While a student at DePaul University College of Law, Mr. Koenig was a member of Moot Court and took first place in the all-school Negotiations Competition.

APPENDICES

APPENDIX A

PLANNING FOR THE FUTURE - LIVING TRUSTS, ESTATE, AND TAX PLANNING

A. OVERVIEW

1. Why is estate planning necessary generally?

a. Unless you decide to whom you would like your assets to pass at your death, the State of Illinois will make the decision for you

i. The Illinois Probate Act sets forth a priority of distribution for individuals who die "intestate" (without a will or trust);

ii. The statutory scheme may not be what you intend, or even what you would expect;

iii. It is not true, however, that if you die without a will your property automatically will pass to the State (unless you have absolutely **no** relatives living).

b. Unless you die with a will or trust in existence, the State will also decide who has the right to administer your estate

i. The statute generally gives priority to relatives in the order of closeness (i.e., first your spouse, then your children, etc.) — The individual having priority, however, may not be the best person for the job (i.e., your spouse or children might have absolutely no investment experience or may be "spendthrifts" who are unable to manage their own funds);

ii. If you establish a will or trust, you decide who should manage your estate — you may decide to use an unrelated individual (such as your accountant or investment counselor) or even a bank, having more experience in these matters.

c. As a general rule, the costs associated with administering an intestate estate are greater than if you die with a will or trust

i. The administrator of an intestate estate is required by law to post a bond with corporate surety in an amount equal to 1-1/2 times the value of your estate:

(a) The surety bond premium charged is generally 1 to 2 percent of the amount of the bond (i.e., for a $500,000 estate, the required bond would be $750,000 (1-1/2 times), so the premium could be in excess of $10,000 annually);

(b) With a will or trust on the other hand, surety on the bond can be waived, thus decreasing the cost.

ii. Where a large number of statutory "heirs" are involved, the general administration of the estate and the time expended by the estate's attorney tend to be greater, thus increasing cost.

d. Without a will or trust, there is absolutely no opportunity for planning for the minimization of Federal and state estate tax (discussed below).

e. Moreover, in an intestate situation, there is no opportunity for planning for special circumstances, such as a minor or disabled child, or a "spendthrift" child who cannot properly manage funds.

i. With a will or trust, you can provide that a beneficiary's share is to be held in trust, with a trustee making decisions as to the beneficiary's need, and/or you can provide for the beneficiary's inheritance to be held in trust until a more mature age;

ii. In an intestate estate, all property would simply be distributed outright to your heirs, except in the case of a minor, in which case a guardianship estate might need to be opened for the minor, or the minor's share might need to be held in a special bank account subject to further order of Court until the child reaches legal age.

f. Without a will, the Court will decide upon the appropriate guardian for any minor children.

2. "Living trust" vs. will — Which is right for you?

a. What is a "living trust"?

i. You establish a trust agreement currently, naming yourself (usually) or a third party as trustee;

ii. After establishing the trust, title to your various assets is re-registered in the name of the trustee (this is known as the process of trust "funding");

iii. During your lifetime and so long as you are competent, you retain full control over all trust assets, and retain the right to amend or revoke the trust at any time;

iv. If you should become incompetent during your lifetime, the trustee (or the successor trustee designated in the trust if you were acting as your own trustee) would manage the assets and make distributions for your benefit;

v. Upon your death, the trustee or successor trustee, as the case may be, pays all debts, taxes, and expenses, and then administers and distributes all remaining property as provided in the trust — thus, the trust in effect substitutes for a traditional will.

b. Advantages of a living trust over a traditional will

i. Assuming the trust is fully funded at your death (i.e., title to all property has been changed over to the trustee), probate proceedings will be avoided at your death

(a) The expense of probate court proceedings and fees relating thereto can be avoided;

(b) Since a trust is not required to be filed with any court, your financial affairs and the beneficiaries of your estate remain confidential — In a probate proceeding, on the other hand, your will is a public document, available for anyone to see;

(c) Your assets are immediately available to pay expenses and make distributions to family members if appropriate — In a probate proceeding, the assets are tied up for a minimum of six months, until the expiration of the statutory claims period for creditors.

ii. Similarly, if you should become incompetent during your lifetime, guardianship proceedings may be avoided, again assuming a properly funded trust

(a) The trustee would be given authority in the trust to manage the trust and make distributions for your benefit, without court involvement or supervision;

(b) Guardianship proceedings are particularly expensive, as almost all actions taken by the guardian, must receive prior approval by the Court;

(c) Again, privacy is maintained, and perhaps dignity which might otherwise be lost in a public guardianship proceeding may be maintained.

c. Disadvantages of living trust over traditional will

i. Up front legal cost of drafting of living trust is somewhat greater than for a traditional will — however, the difference in cost should not be substantial, and is more than offset by the cost savings in the future through probate avoidance (and possible estate tax savings, as discussed below)

ii. Care and time must be taken after the trust is established to transfer title to your various assets to the trustee

(a) The paperwork up front is again worth the savings down the line, however;

(b) Assuming you act as your own trustee, the fact that the title to your assets would now be in the name of the trust should not be a deterrent to establishing the trust;

(c) In the event that all assets are not transferred into the trust, you would use a "pour over" will in conjunction with the trust to ensure that all assets ultimately end up in the trust.

B. BASIC ESTATE TAX PLANNING

1. For those individuals who expect to have assets at death valued in excess of the Federal estate tax "applicable exemption amount" (or who are close to the threshold amount), planning steps should be

taken to avoid or minimize the Federal and Illinois estate tax.

a. The "applicable exemption amount" has currently been repealed, but subject to further legislation, this repeal will only last for one year, at which time the applicable exemption amount will revert to the prior law amount of $1,000,000 in 2011.

b. In this regard, the proceeds of any life insurance policies and employee benefits should be considered, as well as the value of any real estate, stocks, bonds, bank accounts or other assets;

c. Without proper planning, estate tax may unnecessarily be paid, thus reducing the amount passing to your heirs;

d. The current estate tax brackets are repealed but effective in 2011 may be as high as 55 percent — consequently, the tax exposure may be substantial.

2. **In planning for estate tax minimization, two concepts are key — the applicable exemption amount and the unlimited marital deduction**.

a. Assuming the applicable exemption amount reverts to $1,000,000, each individual may give away up to the applicable exemption amount at his or her death without paying any estate tax. The amount of this exemption is set forth above;

b. In addition, for married individuals, an unlimited marital deduction is allowed at the first death for any property which passes to the survivor, regardless of amount;

i. Example: Husband owns $2,000,000 worth of assets, all held in joint tenancy with Wife. Upon Husband's death, all property passes to Wife. No tax is payable as a result of Husband's death due to the unlimited marital deduction (BUT WHAT HAPPENS ON WIFE'S DEATH?... SEE BELOW);

ii. The unlimited marital deduction is not available, however, if the surviving spouse is not a United States citizen (even though a resident alien), unless a special type of trust, known as a QDOT, is established;

iii. Any existing wills or trusts executed before 1982 should be reviewed, as substantial changes in the estate tax law have occurred, and the unlimited marital deduction may not be available for those documents, unless revised.

3. Combining the applicable exemption amount and the unlimited marital deduction to minimize estate tax for married couples.

a. In most marital situations, there is a tendency to leave all property outright to the surviving spouse, or to hold title to all assets jointly;

i. From a tax planning standpoint, this is **not** recommended, as it generally will not result in estate tax minimization (assuming combined assets in excess of the applicable exemption amount);

(a) Although there will be no tax at the first death due to the unlimited marital deduction, the applicable exemption amount of the first spouse will be wasted — thus, at the second death, only an amount equal to that spouse's own exemption will be sheltered from tax;

(b) In the above Example, although no tax is payable upon Husband's death, at Wife's death she will have a taxable estate of $2,000,000, and (assuming death occurs after 2010) will only have $1,000,000 of exemption available to shelter her estate from tax. Thus, estate tax at Wife's death will be payable on $1,000,000, with a tax liability payable to the IRS possibly as much as $550,000, reducing the amount passing to the children.

b. The tax preferred approach would be the use of a Marital Trust/Family Trust arrangement — Here's how it works:

i. The estate plan of each spouse provides that upon the first spouse's death, an amount equal to the deceased spouse's unused applicable exemption amount is to be allocated to a separate trust known as the "Family Trust" — This trust is designed to shelter the deceased spouse's exemption amount from tax.

(a) The surviving spouse may receive benefits from this trust including any one or more of the following:

(1) The right to receive all income;

(2) The right to receive principal from the trust for the survivor's health, support and maintenance;

(3) A "power of appointment," allowing the survivor to rearrange the ultimate distribution of the trust in favor of anyone other than the spouse, the spouse's estate, the spouse's creditors, or the creditors of the spouse's estate; and

(4) The unlimited right to withdraw the larger of $5,000 or 5 percent of the value of the trust each year, for any reason.

(b) The survivor may also act as his or her own trustee, and consequently could make decisions on his or her own behalf;

(c) The tax advantage of this arrangement is that upon the survivor's death, no portion of the Family Trust will be included in his or her tax base, and consequently the property of this trust will pass tax-free to the children or other beneficiaries.

ii. To the extent that the assets of the deceased spouse exceed the applicable exemption amount, any excess assets would be allocated to the Marital Trust

(a) The trust is designed to qualify for the unlimited marital deduction, to ensure that no tax will be payable at the first spouse's death;

(b) This trust will be taxable in the survivor's estate at his or her death, but he or she may apply his or her own exemption against this trust, as well as the survivor's own assets;

(c) Since the Marital Trust will be taxable in the survivor's estate, the survivor can be given an unlimited right of withdrawal or general power of appointment over this trust, or this portion can be distributed outright to the survivor.

iii. The net result of the Marital Trust/Family Trust arrangement is that an amount equal to <u>both</u> spouses' applicable exemption amount can effectively be sheltered from estate tax after both spouses' deaths, with minimal restrictions having been placed on the survivor's access to funds during his or her lifetime.

iv. <u>Example</u>: In the previous Example, if Husband had a $2,000,000 estate and had a will or trust which provided for the

1. foregoing arrangement, the result would be as follows: Upon Husband's death, the first $1,000,000 would be allocated to the Family Trust, and would be sheltered from tax by Husband's exemption. The remaining $1,000,000 would be allocated to the Marital Trust, and would qualify for the unlimited marital deduction. Thus, no tax would be payable at Husband's death. Wife would receive benefits from both the Marital Trust and the Family Trust during her lifetime, but upon her death only the Marital Trust would be taxable in her estate. Assuming no other assets, Wife's taxable estate is $1,000,000, but she applies her own exemption against this amount, resulting in no tax being payable at her death. Thus, the entire $2,000,000 passes to the children tax-free, saving the estate tax which would have been payable if all property had been owned jointly or had passed directly to Wife at Husband's death.

v. Note: The Marital Trust is also sometimes referred to in literature as "Trust A" or the "Spouse's Trust", and the Family Trust is sometimes known as "Trust B" or the "Exemption Trust" or the "Shelter Trust" — whatever the terminology used, the net result is the same.

C. ADVANCED ESTATE PLANNING TECHNIQUES

1. Irrevocable Life Insurance Trusts.

a. For individuals having substantial amounts of life insurance, this device may effectively remove the proceeds of life insurance from the estate tax base **altogether**;

b. Irrevocable nature of the document requires careful thought as to provisions contained therein;

c. For existing insurance policies, effectiveness of tax avoidance depends upon whether owner of policies survives for three years after policies are transferred to the trust.

2. Generation-Skipping Transfer Tax Planning.

a. For individuals having estates valued at more than $1,000,000, a generation-skipping trust can effectively reduce estate tax at the level of the next generation (i.e., at your child's death);

b. Basically, trust is designed to continue through life of first generation (i.e., child), with benefits being available to that beneficiary, if needed, but not vesting in the beneficiary and upon the beneficiary's death distributing to the next generation (i.e., grandchildren);

c. Since trust never vests in first generation, the trust is not includable in the estate of the first generation beneficiary at death, but instead passes tax-free to the next generation;

d. Usefulness of this device depends upon size of your estate and likelihood that your children or other first generation beneficiaries will have their own estate tax exposure (i.e., that their estates at their deaths will be larger than the applicable exemption amount);

D. LIVING WILLS AND HEALTH CARE POWERS OF ATTORNEY

1. **A "living will" or declaration is a document whereby you indicate your desire not to be maintained on life support procedures if you are suffering from an incurable and terminal condition, and would not be able to survive but for such procedures.**

   a. The decision to "pull the plug" is ultimately left to the physician;

   b. The statute does not **require** any doctor or hospital to withhold or withdraw such procedures, but if he or she refuses to do so, the statute requires that the patient be transferred to another physician who will honor the directive.

2. **A health care power of attorney allows you to appoint an agent to make medical and health care decisions if you are otherwise unable to do so.**

   a. The Illinois statutory form also covers the life support situation, and authorizes the agent to decide whether to withhold or withdraw such procedures in accordance with your wishes as expressed in the health care power of attorney;

   b. On the one hand, the health care power of attorney is more "personal" than the living will, since the designated agent, rather than the doctor, ultimately makes the decision — On the other hand, the health care power of attorney forces your agent to make a very difficult and emotional decision;

   c. The health care power is broader than the living will, since it authorizes all types of medical decisions to be made by the agent if you are unable to do so (for example, if you are unconscious, but not otherwise terminal, your agent could consent to recommended surgery).

d. The health care power and living will are not mutually exclusive (you can have both at the same time). However, if a conflict arises between the two documents, the health care power of attorney will be controlling.

3. **The "food and water" issue — The Nancy Cruzan Case.**

a. As a result of a series of Supreme Court decisions, nutrition and hydration (food and water) may now be withheld or withdrawn as "life support procedures" if there is evidence that you would have desired such;

b. In view of the cases, it is best if you specifically indicate in your living will or health care power of attorney whether or not you intend for food and water to be considered to be "life support" procedures which may be withheld or withdrawn under appropriate circumstances.

This document provides information on current legal issues. However, that information should not be construed as an opinion as to particular situations or applications.

Pursuant to Internal Revenue Service Circular No. 230, be advised that this advice was not intended or written to be used, and it cannot be used by any taxpayer, for the purpose of avoiding any Internal Revenue Code penalties that may be imposed on the taxpayer. The advice was written to support the promotion or marketing of the transaction(s) or matter(s) addressed by the written advice. The taxpayer should seek advice based on the taxpayer's particular circumstances from an independent tax advisor.

Courtesy of Colleen Chinlund, Arnstein & Lehr LLP

APPENDIX B

SAMPLE SETTLEMENT AGREEMENT AND MUTUAL GENERAL RELEASE

This Settlement Agreement and Mutual General Release (the "Agreement") is made and entered into as of ____________, 2010 ("Effective Date") by and between Party 1, on the one hand, and Party 2, individually, and as trustee of the Trust, dated __________ (the "Trust") (in either or both capacities herein referred to as "Party 2"), on the other hand. Party 1 and Party 2 are hereinafter individually referred to as a "Party," and collectively referred to as the "Parties."

<u>R E C I T A L S</u>

WHEREAS,

WHEREAS,

WHEREAS,

WHEREAS,

WHEREAS, the Parties desire to settle all disputes between them as described above, and any and all other disputes, without the expense of further litigation.

<u>**A G R E E M E N T**</u>

NOW, THEREFORE, the Parties hereby agree as follows:

1. **<u>Settlement Payment</u>**. Party 2 agrees to pay Party 1, by wire transfer to the ________________________________ Client Trust Account, the sum of $________________.

2. The Parties shall bear their own costs and attorneys' fees arising out of or related to this matter.

3. **Dismissal of Application**.

(a) Promptly upon the full execution and exchange of this Agreement by the Parties and their attorneys, and transfer of the Settlement Payments, counsel for Party 1 shall file a Request for Dismissal with prejudice as to the Application and Petition.

(b) The Parties agree that the above-referenced Court shall retain jurisdiction to enforce this Agreement pursuant to Code of Civil Procedure § 664.6 or other appropriate legal means.

4. **Mutual General Releases**

(a) Except for the obligations set forth in this Agreement, Party 1, and each of them, for themselves and on behalf of any and all persons and/or entities who may purport to claim by or through them (collectively, the "Party 1 Releasors"), will and hereby do release and forever discharge Party 2, individually, as trustee of the Trust, and each of their respective agents, employees, attorneys and representatives (herein collectively referred to as the "Party 2 Releasees"), and each of them, from any and all claims, debts, damages, liabilities, demands, obligations, costs, expenses, disputes, actions and causes of action of every nature, whether known or unknown, suspected or unsuspected, which the Party 1 Releasors, and each or any of them, now hold or have at any time heretofore owned or held against the Party 2 Releasees, including without limitation, any claims or causes of action arising out of, based upon or related to the Application and Petition.

(b) Except for the obligations set forth in this Agreement, Party 2, for each of themselves individually, as trustee of the Trust, and on behalf of any and all persons and/or entities who may purport to claim by or through any of them (collectively, the "Party 2 Releasors"), will and hereby does release and forever discharge Party 1, and each of them, and each of their respective agents, employees, attorneys and representatives (herein collectively referred to as the "Party 1 Releasees"), and each of them, from any and all claims, debts, damages, liabilities, demands, obligations, costs, expenses, disputes, actions and causes of action of every nature, whether known or unknown, suspected or unsuspected, which the Party 2 Releasors, and each or any of them, now hold or have at any time heretofore owned or held against the Party 1 Releasees, including without limitation, any claims or causes of action arising out of, based upon or related to the Application and Petition.

(c) The Parties hereby acknowledge and agree that the foregoing mutual releases expressly exclude the release of any rights or obligations created under this Agreement.

(d) The Parties hereby covenant and agree not to institute or prosecute any action or proceeding based on any of the claims that are released or intended to be released by this Agreement, or which are otherwise referred to herein.

5. **Waiver of Civil Code Section 1542**

It is the intention of Party 1, and each of them, on the one hand, and Party 2, on the other hand, in executing this Agreement and receiving the consideration called for herein, that this Agreement be and is effective as a full and final accord and satisfaction and mutual release of all claims, debts, damages, liabilities, demands, obligations, costs, expenses, disputes, actions and causes of action, known or unknown, suspected or unsuspected, between the Parties that are expressly released herein. In furtherance of this intention, Party 1 and Party 2, and each of them, hereby acknowledge that they are familiar with California Civil Code § 1542 and that they hereby waive and relinquish any right or benefit which they have or may have under that section, which provides as follows:

> A GENERAL RELEASE DOES NOT EXTEND TO CLAIMS WHICH THE CREDITOR DOES NOT KNOW OR SUSPECT TO EXIST IN HIS OR HER FAVOR AT THE TIME OF EXECUTING THE RELEASE, WHICH IF KNOWN BY HIM OR HER MUST HAVE MATERIALLY AFFECTED HIS OR HER SETTLEMENT WITH THE DEBTOR.

6. **Representations and Warranties**

(a) The Parties each represent and warrant to the others that they own the claims released herein, that none of the claims released herein have been assigned to any other person or entity and that no other person or entity has any interest with respect to the claims released herein.

(b) The Parties each represent and warrant to the others that none of them nor any of their respective agents, representatives or attorneys nor any other person or entity in order to induce any of the Parties to enter into this Agreement have made any promise, assurance, representation, inducement or warranty whatsoever, whether express or implied or statutory, which is not specifically set forth in writing in this Agreement and further acknowledge that this Agreement has not been entered into in reliance upon any promise, assurance, representation, inducement or warranty not expressly set forth in writing in this Agreement.

(c) The Parties each represent and warrant to the others that they have received independent legal advice from their respective attorneys with respect to the advisability of making the settlement provided for herein, with respect to the advisability of executing this Agreement and with respect to the advisability of waiving any rights conferred by the provisions of California Civil Code § 1542.

(d) The Parties each represent and warrant to the others that he/she/it has the authority to enter into this Agreement, that any person executing this Agreement in a representative capacity is duly authorized to do so, and each person executing this Agreement in a representative capacity represents, warrants and covenants that he or she is duly authorized to do so pursuant to appropriate bylaw or resolution or other authority.

(e) The Parties each represent and warrant to the others that they have read and understand this Agreement and that this Agreement is executed voluntarily and without duress or undue influence on the part of or on behalf of any party hereto. The Parties hereby acknowledge that they have been represented in the negotiations and preparation of this Agreement by counsel of their own choice, and that they have read this Agreement and had it fully explained to them by such counsel, and that they are fully aware of the contents of this Agreement and of the legal effect of each and every provision herein.

7. **Enforcement of Agreement**

If any Party brings an action arising out of or to enforce this Agreement, including without limitation, the filing of a motion to enforce this Agreement under Code of Civil Procedure § 664.6, the prevailing party shall be entitled to recover its costs and expenses, including all court costs and attorneys' fees, if any, incurred in connection with such suit or motion.

8. **Further Assurances**

Time is of the essence of each and every provision of this Agreement. The Parties shall each execute any and all other documents and take any and all further steps which may be necessary or appropriate to further or implement the terms of this Agreement.

9. **Construction of Agreement**

This Agreement shall be construed as a whole in accordance with its fair meaning and in accordance with the laws of the State of California. The language of this Agreement shall not be construed for or against any particular party as each of the Parties' attorneys has assisted in the drafting of this Agreement. The headings used herein are for reference only and shall not affect the construction of this Agreement.

10. **Sole Agreement**

This Agreement represents the sole and entire agreement between the Parties and supersedes all prior agreements, negotiations and discussions between the Parties hereto and/or their respective counsel with respect to the subject matters covered hereby.

11. **Amendment to Agreement**

Any amendment to this Agreement must be in a writing signed by duly authorized representatives of the Parties hereto and stating the intent of the Parties to amend this Agreement.

12. **Counterparts**

This Agreement may be executed in one or more counterparts, each of which shall be deemed an original, but all of which shall together constitute but one and the same instrument. Fax or email signatures shall be deemed sufficient to make this Agreement binding.

IN WITNESS WHEREOF, the Parties hereto have executed this Agreement as of the date set forth above as follows:

____
PARTY 1

____
PARTY 2

Approved as to form:

DATED: ________________ ______________________________
____
Attorney for Party 1

DATED: ________________ ______________________________
____
Attorney for Party 2

Courtesy of Scott A. Harshman, Jeffer Mangels Butler & Mitchell LLP

APPENDIX C

DOCUMENT EXECUTION CHECKLIST

Date: ______________

Questionnaire For Execution of Estate Planning Documents

Client:

Testator:

Client/Matter No.:

		Yes	No
1.	Have you examined and do you approve these documents?	[ ]	[ ]
2.	Do these documents accurately reflect your wishes regarding the disposition of your property upon your death?	[ ]	[ ]
3.	Do you have any questions about these documents?	[ ]	[ ]
4.	Have you recently had any drug, alcohol or other substance which would influence your thought processes?	[ ]	[ ]
5.	Has anyone placed any pressure, duress or other influence upon you regarding any of these documents?	[ ]	[ ]
6.	Is this document intended to be your ______________?	[ ]	[ ]
7.	Do you want us to witness your ________________?	[ ]	[ ]

Additional Information:

____

Attorney Supervising Execution:_______________________

Initials of Supervising Attorney:_______________________

Courtesy of Scott A. Harshman, Jeffer Mangels Butler & Mitchell LLP

APPENDIX D

CHECKLIST FOR ESTATE LITIGATION

I. Intake

1. What time deadlines are relevant?
2. What documents do I need for initial review?
3. What information does the client have at this stage?

II. Preliminary Analysis

1. What claims/defenses are appropriate?
2. What evidence supports these claims/defenses?

    a. Witnesses
    b. Documents
    c. e-discovery
    d. Medical evidence
    e. Other

3. What is my best case scenario and worst case scenario on the facts available at present?
4. What jurisdictions are available and what are their advantages?
5. What judge is likely to be assigned to this case and can I take a change of judge if necessary?
6. What tax issues are presented, if any?
7. Is there an in terrorem clause if this is a contest?
8. What are the other side's likely defenses/claims?
9. Is a counterclaim likely?
10. What is the staffing and budget for this case?
11. Have I made sure that my firm has no conflicts?
12. Should I use a private investigator before filing suit?
13. Are all necessary parties included or is there virtual representation available?

III. Commencing the Suit (or the defense)

1. Filing Fee.
2. Arrange for service and monitor status of service.
3. Calendar default deadlines if Plaintiff.
4. Focus on Answer deadlines and other time limitations.
5. Will the case be treated like a regular civil case or do I need to take further action to insure all rules apply? [1]
6. Do I need or want to make a jury demand or seek removal to federal court?
7. Will there be equitable clean-up if I have mixed equitable and legal claims?
8. Have all necessary parties been included?
9. Have I pled damages appropriately?
10. Have I pled all the elements of each claim or defense?

IV. Discovery

1. File paper discovery – document requests and interrogatories including especially ID of experts, damages and witnesses.
2. Do I need to subpoena third parties?
3. Make sure business records requirements are satisfied early on. (e.g. obtain business records affidavit and forward all to opposing counsel)
4. Do I need to send a letter asking that electronic evidence be preserved?
5. Do I need to engage an e-discovery or handwriting expert?
6. What witnesses do I need to depose and in what order?
7. What witnesses do I need to interview?
8. Do I need to use a private investigator?
9. Do I need to address questionable discovery objections?

[1] In some jurisdictions, cases filed in probate court are not governed by all of the normal rules of civil procedure. In a substantial case the safeguards and greater certainty provided by such rules is usually preferred. A motion to apply all of the rules to a probate case can often be filed as a matter of course.

V. TRIAL PREPARATION

1. Organize file.
2. Evaluate all evidence and information adduced.
3. Advise client of risks and other important issues.
4 Should I attempt to settle?
5. Is mediation appropriate?
6. Analyze depositions and highlight key portions
7. Organize exhibits
8. Outline witness order.
9. Witness preparation.
10. Prepare for cross examination
11. Are motions in limine appropriate?
12. Research and prepare for any expected evidentiary issues.
13. Do I need a jury consultant?
14. Do I need audio-visual assistance?
15. Prepare jury instructions. Any special interrogatories?
16. Prepare for voir dire, (if jury)
17. Prepare opening statement
18. If bench trial – do I need to request any specific findings prior to commencing the trial?[2]

VI. Trial

1. Voir Dire (if jury)
2. Opening Statement
3. Present Evidence.
4. If defendant, prepare a motion for directed verdict or for judgment.
5. Defense Case
6. Motion for directed verdict or for judgment.
7. Closing statement
8. Verdict—poll jury?
9. If bench trial – any post trial briefing.

[2] In some jurisdictions failure to request specific findings of fact prior to trial may waive the ability to challenge any factual finding on appeal.

VII Post Trial

1. Determine deadlines for post trial motions
2. Determine appeal deadlines
3. File post trial motions if desired – do they preserve all that is needed for appeal?
4 File appeal if desired.
5. Supersedeas Bond?
6. Discovery in aid of collection?
7. Garnishment, execution, levy, etc.

Courtesy of Robert J. Selsor, Polsinelli Shughart PC